Hans von Bülow's Letters to Johannes Brahms

A Research Edition

Edited by Hans-Joachim Hinrichsen
Translated by Cynthia Klohr

THE SCARECROW PRESS, INC.
Lanham • Toronto • Plymouth, UK
2012

Published by Scarecrow Press, Inc.
A wholly owned subsidary of The Rowman & Littlefield Publishing Group, Inc.
4501 Forbes Boulevard, Suite 200, Lanham, Maryland 20706
http://www.scarecrowpress.com

Estover Road, Plymouth PL6 7PY, United Kingdom

Copyright © 2012 by Cynthia Klohr (English language translation)
original German language © Hans-Joachim Hinrichsen
Title of the German original: *Hans von Bülow. Die Briefe an Johannes Brahms.* Published in 1994 by Hans Schneider, Tutzing

Illustrations by permission of the National Library at Berlin, Prussian Cultural Heritage Foundation, Department of Music

British Library Cataloguing in Publication Information Available

Library of Congress Cataloging-in-Publication Data

Bülow, Hans von, 1830–1894.
  [Correspondence. Selections. English]
  Hans von Bülow's letters to Johannes Brahms : a research edition / edited by Hans-Joachim Hinrichsen ; translated by Cynthia Klohr.
      p. cm.
  Originally published: Hans von Bülow. Die Briefe an Johannes Brahms. Tutzing : Hans Schneider, 1994.
  Includes bibliographical references and index.
  ISBN 978-0-8108-8215-7 (cloth : alk. paper) — ISBN 978-0-8108-8216-4 (ebook)
  1. Bülow, Hans von, 1830-1894—Correspondence. 2. Brahms, Johannes, 1833–1897—Correspondence. 3. Conductors (Music)—Germany—Correspondence. 4. Composers—Germany—Correspondence. I. Hinrichsen, Hans-Joachim. II. Title.
  ML422.B9A413 2012
  780.92—dc23
  [B]   2011027009

∞™ The paper used in this publication meets the minimum requirements of American National Standard for Information Sciences—Permanence of Paper for Printed Library Materials, ANSI/NISO Z39.48-1992.

Printed in the United States of America

306981616/

Contents

Foreword to the 1994 German Edition

One hundred years after Hans von Bülow's death, this work presents for the first time a complete and commented edition of his letters to Johannes Brahms. Three final volumes (dating 1904, 1907, and 1908) of the large eight-volume publication of Bülow's correspondence arranged by his widow (parts of which were prepublished in 1907 in *Neue Deutsche Rundschau*) did contain some of Bülow's letters to Brahms. But the edition fails to meet academic standards, as valuable as it may be in general. Its rigorous selection neglected several letters to Brahms. And those that did find their way into the eight volumes are rarely reproduced unabridged. Not every omission was noted, the names of some individuals still living at the time were masked, and even style was sometimes slightly altered. Clearly a new edition is desirable.

For making this edition possible through practical assistance and shared insights I thank Helmut Hell (National Library, Berlin) for permission to publish material; Ute Nawroth and Peter Thüringer (National Library, Berlin) for support in accessing Hans von Bülow's letters and remaining papers, and Herta Müller (National Museum, Meiningen), Peter Cahn (Frankfurt/Main), and Kurt Hofmann (Brahms Institute, Lübeck) for advice on arranging the commentary.

Hans-Joachim Hinrichsen

Preface

$\mathcal{H}$ans von Bülow's letters to Johannes Brahms are kept in the music section of the National Library at Berlin (Building 1, Unter den Linden), which also keeps papers of Bülow's estate inasmuch as Marie von Bülow submitted them in several phases beginning in 1911. Fifty-six letters and one telegram have survived. In 1905 these were returned from Brahms's estate to Bülow's widow. The number of letters originally in Brahms's possession was slightly larger than the bundle of papers now kept in Berlin. We know this from notes on the outside envelope and from correspondence between Brahms's heirs and Marie von Bülow.

Using a preprinted form, Marie von Bülow pledged to a group of heirs represented by Josef Reitzes to protect their proprietary interests and maintain "respect for Brahms or the writer," signed 5 May 1902 (SBB; Sign.: Mus. Ep. H. v. Bülow Varia 4). After formalities were completed and necessary statements affirmed, the sheaf of documents was sent to her on 10 April 1905 by a Viennese notary of the public, who, however, on behalf of the group of heirs represented by Reitzes, requested the return of all papers (letters or enclosures) containing any notes made by Brahms (SBB; Sign.: Mus. Ep. H. v. Bülow Varia 5). The outside envelope holding the letters given to Maria von Bülow, itself not cataloged but kept together with the letters, exhibits several layers of handwritten notes revealing how much of the bundle was returned, probably to fulfill the notary's request:[1] "60 pages thereof / 1 piece including a newspaper clipping / 1 [piece including] a calling card / 1 piece [including] a concert program / 4 [pieces] in an envelope containing a note by Johannes Brahms / 1 small unsigned slip of paper / 1 telegram from Bülow." The final mark, written in Marie von Bülow's handwriting, documents the stock as it is now: "56 letters from Bülow to Brahms / 1 telegram to Joh. Brahms."[2]

All of the letters were written in ink; some letters exhibit additional marks (some in blue pencil) discussed in the commentary. [The German edition presents the correspondence texts word for word based on the hand-written documents, normalizing some of Bülow's idiosyncratic signs and abbreviations.*] The commentary provides information on the persons, events, and matters mentioned in the documents. In some instances it takes a bit of detail to explain the context that renders an otherwise isolated phrase understandable. The commentary provides (in italics) passages from Brahms's replies, inasmuch as they were accessible or have already been published.

At the back of this volume is a list of names indicating the number of the letter(s) in which a name occurs. Roman-type numbers indicate letters and (where applicable) the corresponding commentary. Numbers in italic type indicate that a name is mentioned in the commentary to that letter only. As a rule, information about individuals is provided the first time they appear; in all other cases the relevant commentary note can be easily found by consulting the index.

NOTES

1. The entry for the epistles' inventory to Brahms's estate also reads "60 Letters from Hans von Bülow," cf. Alfred von Ehrmann, *Johannes Brahms: Weg, Werk und Welt* (Leipzig, 1933), p. 446.

2. The little unsigned scrap of paper mentioned in the oldest inventory still exists, but its significance is unclear. On it Bülow wrote, "Euripides can arrive just before the performance and return immediately afterward to Bamberg, where the hotel near the train station has good beds. / Perhaps the enclosed coupon for a visit to reserved rooms in the restaurant there (drinks not included) may persuade him" (Sign.: Mus. ep. H. v. Bülow Varia 7). "Euripides" is a nickname Bülow sometimes used for Brahms (see commentary to letter no. 14).

---

*For the English rendition, some abbreviations have been written out to facilitate readability.

Introduction

Hans von Bülow (1830–1894)
and Johannes Brahms (1833–1897)

$\mathcal{T}$he correspondence between Hans von Bülow and Johannes Brahms that has been preserved commences in the autumn of 1877, when Bülow was forty-seven and Brahms forty-four, and it continues until the autumn of 1892. By the time their exchange of letters began, the two had already been acquainted for years; thus it helps to understand their relationship if we examine its earlier phases more carefully. Hans Guido Baron von Bülow was born on 8 January 1830 in Dresden into a family whose lifestyle, despite nobility and heritage, was that of the cultured and educated middle class. Hans's father, Eduard von Bülow, himself a well-received author and close friend of Ludwig Tieck, pursued a broad literary upbringing for his son; the child learned to speak French as fluently as German. Hans's mother, Francisca (née Stoll), was related by marriage to the upper-class Frege family in Leipzig where, during one of his many holiday visits, the boy also met Mendelssohn. Destined early for a diplomatic career, Hans showed no particular signs of musical talent for years. Following several bouts of meningitis, however, some of which were life threatening, at the age of nine it was discovered that he had profound musicality, and systematic instruction in music was arranged. As the proven Bülow family legend goes, at the age of twelve, on 19 October 1842, Hans experienced the premier performance of *Rienzi* at the Dresden court opera and it awakened him. He finished school in the spring of 1848 in Stuttgart, where the family had moved (for reasons unknown) in mid-1846. By far the greatest reward of Hans's youth in Stuttgart was a quickly made lifelong friendship with composer Joachim Raff, eight years his senior.

In 1848 Hans von Bülow took up the study of law in Leipzig that he then continued in 1849 in Berlin. Meanwhile music had come to the fore; it meant more to him than any part of his overall education. As early as 1846,

Mittwoch, den 1. März 1854.

Im Apollo-Saale:

Grosse
musikalisch-deklamatorische Soirée

von

Adele Peroni-Glassbrenner.

PROGRAMM.

Erster Theil.

1. "*Blumenglöckchen*," Terzett von *Reissiger*, vorgetragen von den Damen *Fanny* und *Adele Cornet* und *Bertha Holm*.
2. "*Charlotte Ackermann*," Gedicht von *Rud. Gottschall* (Manuscr.), vorgetragen von *Adele Peroni-Glassbrenner*.
3. *Recitativ und Arie* aus "Jakob und seine Söhne," von *Mehul*, vorgetragen von dem Herzogl. Braunschw. Hof-Opernsänger, Herrn *Franz Himmer*.
4. *Erster Satz* aus der *C-dur-Sonate* von *Johannes Brahms*, vorgetragen von dem Pianisten, Herrn *H. v. Bülow*.
5. *Grosse Arie* aus "Il Giuramento," von *Mercadante*, vorgetragen von der Königl. Hannov. Hof- und Kammersängerin, Frau *Madelaine Nottes*.
6. "*Fliegendes Blatt*," von *Grädener*,
   Andante finale de la Lucia, von *Fr. Liszt*, } vorgetragen von
   Valse Impromptu, von *Fr. Liszt*, } Herrn *H. v. Bülow*.
7. "*Ade, du lieber Tannenwald*," Lied von } vorgetragen
   H. Esser, } von Herrn
   "Sei mir gegrüsst!" Lied von *Fr. Schubert*, } *Franz Himmer*.

Zweiter Theil.

8. "*Liebesqual*" und "*Die Auserwählte*," Quartette von *Fr. Kücken*, vorgetragen von den Damen *Franziska*, *Fanny* und *Adele Cornet* und *B. Holm* und vier Herren.
9. "*La Serenata*," Duett von *Rossini*, vorgetragen von Frau *Madelaine Nottes* und Herrn *Franz Himmer*.
10. (Auf vielfaches Begehren:) *Hochzeitsmarsch und Elfenreigen* aus *Mendelssohn's* Musik zum "Sommernachtstraum," für Pianoforte von *Fr. Liszt*, vorgetragen von Herrn *H. v. Bülow*.
11. *Komisches Duett* aus "Chiara di Rosemberg," von *Ricci*, vorgetragen von Herrn *Santerre* und einem Dilettanten.
12. "*Eine Gardinenpredigt*," komisches Zeitgedicht von *Ad. Glassbrenner* (Manuscr.), vorgetragen von *Adele Peroni-Glassbrenner*.
13. "*Das erste Veilchen*," Lied von *Fr. Mendelssohn*, } vorgetragen von
    "*Trockne Blumen*," Lied von *Fr. Schubert*, } Frau *Madelaine*
    "*Waldvöglein*," Lied mit Piano und obligatem } *Nottes* u. Herrn
    Violoncell, } *G. d'Arien*.

Langhoff'sche Buchdruckerei.

Bülow's first public Brahms performance, Hamburg 1854. Ink and pencil marks are by Bülow. *Staatsbibliothek zu Berlin—Preussischer Kulturbesitz; SBB Mus. Db 1815-1 Rara*

before moving to Stuttgart, he had shown some of his own compositions to Richard Wagner in Dresden and gotten explicit encouragement. As a pupil in Stuttgart, Bülow performed publicly at the piano. In the summer of 1849, at the close of his year of study in Leipzig, he visited Franz Liszt in Weimar. He went there again in 1850 at Liszt's invitation to attend the enthusiastically awaited première of *Lohengrin* on 28 August. Bülow then traveled to Switzerland to spend the semester break with his father, who had been divorced in 1849 and planned to remarry. Here the crucial events occurred that were to become almost legendary in the lives of Wagner and Bülow.

While at his father's Swiss residence, Hans von Bülow was summoned by Richard Wagner, who was convinced of the young man's talent since their first encounter in Dresden in 1846 and now urgently sought an assistant conductor for Zurich's orchestra. The commotion heightening the choice has often been told—Bülow's clandestine flight from his father's home to Wagner, then falling on his knees before his father, who had come after him but was eventually persuaded to let his son pursue a career in music. And just as that busy season in Switzerland, first in Zurich under the direction of Wagner and then in St. Gallen on his own at the city theater, set the cornerstone for Bülow's later work as a conductor, so too was the concert pianist Hans von Bülow shaped by Franz Liszt, to whom Wagner recommended him in 1851.

In Weimar, Bülow renewed his friendship with Joachim Raff, who meanwhile assisted Liszt there. He also became at first close friends with Joseph Joachim, concertmaster of the Weimar orchestra. Joseph Joachim left Weimar in 1853, the same year Bülow did, to become concertmaster in Hanover. In March, Bülow began in Vienna his career as a pianist, equipped with a recommendation by Liszt, who openly proclaimed him his "legitimate heir." That career attempt, however, was not entirely successful.

It was Bülow's friendship with Joseph Joachim that led him to meet Johannes Brahms. Bülow had missed Brahms's visit with Liszt in Weimar because at the time he was giving concerts in Austria and Hungary, not returning to Germany until the late summer of 1853. But he did carefully read Schumann's article on Brahms titled "Neue Bahnen" (New Paths) in the *Neue Zeitschrift für Musik* (New Journal of Music), dated 28 October 1853. Bülow's letter to Liszt dated 5 November 1853 contains his first extant mention of Brahms: "Mozart-Brahms ou Schumann-Brahms ne trouble point du tout la tranquillité de mon sommeil. J'attendrai ses manifestions."[1] The controversial ambivalent effect wrought by Schumann's article—more a burden than a boon for Brahms—is evidenced by Bülow's reaction. Before meeting Brahms personally, Bülow wrote for the *New Journal of Music* a review of Joachim Raff's piano piece *Frühlingsboten* (Signs of Spring), op. 55. The article began with an ironic poke at Schumann's Brahms propaganda: "Spring is an old friend;

it doesn't change signs and while the paths it takes are fresh and green, they are not brand new."[2] To Raff, Bülow joked about "the Hindu oracle from Dusseldorf."[3] Then, while visiting Joseph Joachim, he finally met Brahms in person. By this time Bülow's article had already been published, but now Bülow was, in several respects, no longer uninformed: Schumann's article had aroused in him a cautious curiosity full of expectation, marked by irony and skepticism. His friend Joachim's reports further piqued his interest. And finally, Bülow had been prepared for the encounter with Brahms in Hanover by a letter from Liszt, dated 16 December 1853. Liszt had just met the composer for the second time that year in Leipzig and studied the galley proofs of Brahms's Sonata in C major for the piano:[4]

> Vous y [= at Joachim's] trouverez Brahms auquel je m'intéresse sincère-ment et qui s'est conduit avec tact et bon goût envers moi durant les quelques jours que je viens de passer à Leipzig en l'honneur de Berlioz. Aussi l'ai-je invité plusieurs fois á dîner et me plais á croire que ses "neue Bahnen" le rapprocheront davantage de Weymar par la suit. Vous serez content de sa sonate en ut [= op. 1] dont j'ai parcouru les épreuves á Leipzig et qu'il m'avait déjà montrée ici. C'est précisément celui de ses ouvrages qui m'avait donné la meilleure idée de son talent de composition.

When Brahms finally arrived in Hanover in the first days of January, Bülow's initial reserve became wholehearted acceptance: "I have gotten to know Robert Schumann's young prophet Brahms fairly well; he has been here a couple of days and is always with us. He's of a very amiable, candid nature and his talent has, in the best sense, something of God's grace about it," Bülow reported to his mother on 6 January 1854.[5] We do not know how many works of the young composer Bülow actually heard or saw at the time, but he found Brahms "a truly enormously rich creative talent."[6] Thus it is not surprising that when the opportunity arose, Bülow had some of Brahms's works performed publicly. It was music that, at the time, Liszt, too, felt might develop toward the musical ideals pursued in Weimar: On 1 March 1854, in a concert given in Hamburg by singer Adele Glassbrenner-Peroni, Bülow played the first movement of Johannes Brahms's Piano Sonata op. 1—a gesture that even thirty years later Brahms still found touching (see commentary to letter no. 35). But that was all, at first.

In hindsight, how strikingly supple was this mid-nineteenth-century constellation of musicians compared to the stiffness with which it is often described. In young Brahms, Liszt saw a potential Weimarian; Bülow and Joachim established their friendship on shared reverence for Liszt; and Bülow—encouraged by Joachim and soon thereafter invited by Schumann—planned to visit Dusseldorf in hopes of significant artistic rapprochement, similar to that evoked by Brahms's visit a few months before.[7] It was Schumann's sudden and unexpected exiting the constellation in February 1854 that upset the delicate balance. At first the loss had an unintentional and seemingly insignificant side effect: Joachim was no longer available to join Bülow in concerts because he now felt obligated to assist Clara Schumann. By year's end Bülow's relationship with Joachim showed signs of serious strain. Joseph Joachim and Clara Schumann announced their own soirée in Berlin for the very day of Bülow's concert, luring away his audience. Then Joachim turned down Bülow's request to perform together, knowing that Bülow relied on appearing with an already famous musician.[8] The dissonance rose when in August 1857 J. Joachim wrote a now well-known dismissal to Liszt following the publication of Liszt's *Symphonische Dichtungen* (Symphonic Poems), causing Bülow to all the more resolutely side with Liszt.[9]

Opinions gradually became irreconcilable on all sides, and Bülow himself contributed to the unease. In April 1855 he took up at Stern Conservatory in Berlin a position as piano instructor offered to him by Adolph Bernhard Marx. Although what Bülow dubbed his "extreme progressiveness" met with a fair amount of resistance, his new position allowed him to pursue novel musical activities:[10] He aspired to create a "New German" Berlin through involvement in concerts given by the Stern Orchestra Association (and subsequently by the newly founded "Society of the Friends of Music") and by organizing soirées for piano and chamber music.[11] At first young Bülow did not lose sight of Brahms, although he had not again publicly performed Brahms pieces since that sole concert in Hamburg in 1854. On the contrary, upon request, Bülow sent to Jessie Laussot, a friend from school days in Dresden, "a short list of nonconventional piano music." He would suggest, he wrote, "first of all everything by the two composers Rubinstein and Brahms. And then . . . by myself" (13 June 1856).[12] Publicly, however, Bülow had already repositioned "broody Brahms" beneath Anton Rubinstein, whose virtuoso compositions seemed effortless.[13]

Bülow's attitude toward Brahms became one of disapproval following the publication of a manifesto initiated by the latter in the spring of 1860 attacking the New German school. The document was signed by Brahms, Joseph Joachim, Julius Otto Grimm, and Bernhard Scholz. But a mishap let the paper appear prematurely, signed merely by those four and thus robbing it of force. Bülow had been one of the musicians that Brahms and Joachim had hoped would sign it,[14] revealing in retrospect how incompletely Brahms grasped the entire situation. On the other hand, the whole atmosphere was a late symptom of the above-mentioned elasticity pervading the musical-political constellation of the 1850s. The circle broke up following the manifesto. Bülow, at any rate, boasted of having at the last minute persuaded prominent Berlin musicians not to sign.[15] Thereafter he never spoke of Brahms without critical reserve, although in public statements he made an effort to sound impartial. In personal letters Bülow temporarily became so polemic that later the editor of his correspondence omitted passages and altered style out of respect not only for Brahms, but for those other yet-living persons who had signed the manifesto too.[16]

Around this time, Bülow was not only steeped in his emotionally and financially draining artistic propaganda for Berlin; he was also preoccupied more than ever with work for Wagner. In 1859 he painstakingly produced the piano score for *Tristan*, and in 1861 he assisted at *Tannhäuser* rehearsals for Paris. But it was precisely during these years that his youthful "progressiveness" became less radical and his behavior more diplomatic and conciliatory. The way he described the *Allgemeiner Deutscher Musikverein* (*ADMV*; General German Music Association, established in 1861 and seen by the public as an institution of the New German school of music) to Joachim Raff in an attempt to convince him to join, although Raff had long since distanced himself from Liszt, is typical: Many of its members, Bülow wrote, such as

> [Friedrich] Kiel, [Robert] Volkmann, and others, are not of the Weimarian school. Should Brahms and Joachim wish to participate, they, too, will be given opportunities [to perform] at the assembly's concerts. Where, then, is any "imperialistic tendency" to be found—except perhaps within my own person? And do you consider me a purely political musician?[17]

Indeed, although at the time it may have been unintentional, due to his activities in Berlin Bülow had already long been taken for a political musician. The call to Munich in 1864 by Ludwig II, or, more exactly, by Wagner, left that image unaltered.

Bülow's greatest triumph in Munich was surely the première of *Tristan* on 11 June 1865. But by the time Wagner was forced to leave Munich at the end of the year, Bülow's situation had become more unruly than ever. Ensnared in journalistic feuds and private lawsuits, some of which involved his disastrous marriage, and faced with the additional antipathy brought against Prussians in Bavaria following the war of 1866, Bülow left his wife and children waiting with Wagner in Switzerland and returned to Basel in the fall of 1866. From there he initiated in November 1866 a reconciliatory encounter in Mühlhausen with Joachim, whom he hadn't seen in a decade and who was then touring Switzerland and Alsace performing with Brahms. This re-encounter with Brahms no doubt spurred Bülow to peruse the composer's works anew, but his first impression was sober: "to me, it's not music."[18] And yet, in a second proven public endorsement of Brahms, Bülow had Brahms works performed at two of the Basel chamber music soirées: Brahms's Cello

Sonata no. 1, op. 38, on 12 February 1867 and his Horn Trio op. 40 with Hans Richter on 26 March 1867.

In April 1867 a reshuffling of ministers in Munich changed things. Bülow returned to Munich, this time as the royal Bavarian court orchestra conductor and director of the newly established royal school of music. However, after the first performance of *Meistersinger* (Mastersingers) on 21 June 1868, Bülow's Munich career ended abruptly. The emotional strain of trying to hide his yearlong marital crisis from the public and desiring at all costs to avoid quarrel with Richard Wagner took its toll. In September 1869 he submitted his resignation for reasons of health. It was approved, along with continuation of his full salary. A few days earlier his wife Cosima and their children had moved to Wagner's home for good.

Bülow's long retreat to Italy from 1869 to 1872 marks the beginning of a phase of one of the most fundamental transitions in his musical thought. Its most manifest symptom was a cautious approach to Brahms's music. Remarkably, and contrary to belief that Bülow's severe personal disappointment in Richard Wagner influenced his objective judgment, in reality the transition was less linked to alienation from Wagner's works than to the development of an aversion to Liszt's. Bülow's values changed within an intricate yet versatile system, where nothing could be altered without changing something else, and where cause and effect can hardly be distinguished. Without exploring the details, may it suffice to say that Bülow's growing enthusiasm for Brahms had more to do with rediscovering Robert Schumann's work (particularly the late works that Bülow had once dismissed), new appreciation for Mendelssohn, and above all a gradual change in his views on Beethoven's significance for the history of music and the consequences that has for musical interpretation.

From Italy, Bülow began performing as a pianist once again, determined to finance dowries of 40,000 German marks each for his three daughters. (Besides his biological daughters Daniela and Blandine, he had also declared Wagner's daughter Isolde to be his own. After Wagner's death, Bülow claimed paternity for Eva, the youngest, too.) But in the autumn of 1872, after returning to Germany and becoming better acquainted with Brahms in Baden-Baden, Bülow's programs began to include Brahms pieces: some ballads from op. 10; Scherzo op. 4; and Variations on a Theme by Handel op. 24. Bülow took the opportunity to visit Brahms while giving a concert in Vienna on 2 November 1872, although that cannot be considered the commencement of long-standing friendship. Afterward Bülow often performed Robert Schumann's Third Sonata for Piano (op. 14) in the manner that Brahms had reedited it back to having five movements, which is occasionally even explicitly noted in the printed programs.[19] But for many years Brahms's works did not really expand Bülow's repertory. When touring the United States for the first time in 1875–1876, the only Brahms pieces Bülow performed were the Handel Variations op. 24.

This was to change in the autumn of 1877 and the onset of correspondence between Bülow and Brahms marks a new quality in their relationship, one that directly expresses new insights that Bülow gained in interpreting Brahms. For the first time, Bülow planned to rehearse one of Brahms's orchestra compositions, namely the First Symphony, which, after his first acquaintance with it, Bülow immediately began calling "Beethoven's Tenth" (see letter no. 1). Bülow had returned from America in poor health and had been ill for over a year when in his new position as court conductor in Hanover, simultaneously engaged for a series of late fall concerts in Scotland, he met Brahms in Baden-Baden and heard him demonstrate the symphony on the piano. Apparently it was the first time Bülow had heard the piece. On 20 September 1877 he wrote his new superior in Hanover, friend of his youth Hans von Bronsart: "Will consult Brahms today for instruction in performing his symphony (soon in Glasgow). The piece is said to be magnificent."[20] The next day Bülow wrote Bronsart a detailed report on his "consultation with Brahms."[21] We find the exact circumstances of the first time Bülow conducted a Brahms symphony in the first two letters to Brahms and the commentary. But even this act, so very significant for the reestablishment of cordial relations, was not the peak of the development that began in 1872. In retrospect Bülow himself dated his ultimate conversion to Brahms, not incidentally using the metaphor of Paul's conversion at Damascus, at the overwhelming impression he got from the adagio movement of the second symphony (cf. letter no. 42). We don't know when that happened, but he did conduct Brahms's second symphony in Hanover on 26 April 1879.[22]

Bülow's orchestral engagement in Meiningen brought his relationship with Brahms to a new level, changing it from mere acquaintance to personal friendship and intensifying their joint musical efforts. In February 1881 Bülow, who had taken up superintendence of the Meiningen court musicians a few months earlier, gave a Beethoven and Liszt piano recital at the Bösendorfer concert salon in Vienna, and Brahms was present. Afterward, Bülow had an opportunity to tell Brahms about his new principles for working with the Meiningen orchestra—and Brahms perked his ears. He was most intrigued, as Max Kalbeck reports,[23] by Bülow's introduction of separate practice for separate parts. It was a rehearsal reform born out of pure didactic necessity while working on *Tristan and Isolde* in Munich that Bülow was now applying to the fairly insignificant orchestra in Meiningen. There the musicians had few daily obligations and plenty of time for rehearsal, and the reform elevated their technique and teamwork. Bülow suggested that Brahms come and see for himself, and within the summer of the same year, Brahms took up the invitation (see letter no. 3). Upon return from Vienna, Bülow spent considerable rehearsal time expanding the orchestra's repertory for just that purpose: After having devoted the past season to their specialty, namely, the entirety of Beethoven's symphonies, in March 1881 the Meiningen musicians worked predominantly on performing Brahms's first symphony before leaving to earn their livelihood by playing at health resorts and curative water spas during the off-season.[24]

Brahms's friends, who eyed Bülow's activities skeptically, including Clara Schumann and Ferdinand Hiller, were astonished by this nascent cooperation and travel. Brahms felt a need to justify himself and wrote to Ferdinand Hiller in October 1881:[25]

> You, and others, are exaggerating the importance of my "Bülow Trips." I went to Meiningen, above all, to play and try a new piano concerto in peace without the unpleasant prospect of a concert [date]. One would not have found it strange, had I gone anywhere else, even if I had chosen the worst blockhead of a conductor to do it with. Why wonder, then, about [my visiting] Meiningen and Bülow, who admittedly is a very peculiar, disputatious man, but also gifted, serious, and capable? You must realize how thoroughly well his musicians are rehearsed; and then someone like me comes along and works with them as he wishes. Well, I cannot imagine where things could be finer.

Some of Bülow's letters from that period to third parties read like a commentary to his own letters to Brahms no. 4 through 9 because they reveal the emotional pressure brought upon sensitive Bülow by the sheer presence of the composer—particularly because Bülow was unsure whether Brahms was sincere in judging his own (Bülow's) work.[26]

> Master Brahms honored us greatly, but also severely disrupted our work. We had to devote the second week of the month entirely to his works . . . , in order not to make fools of ourselves to his ears. He was here during the third week, coming to rehearsals every day, playing and conducting, performing thrice for the duke himself. There was nothing I could do about it: In an optimistic whirl in Vienna in February I had invited him, and out of respect for his position I felt unable to propose a date that might have been more appropriate for us.—Brahms seemed pleased with himself and spoke often, sometimes quite sarcastically, not simply in praise, but even with delight. He had three dinners at court and was awarded an order of merit, which also seemed to please him. *But I am almost frightened to hear what he tells others, because he is a genius, coequal in "soul" with Richard Wagner.*

> Naturally, his stay enhanced our study of his works; but it did disturb the logical order of our practices and . . . enough said. You may read the rest between the lines, which you know how to do.

This nervousness did not subside until the undertaking had publicly und undeniably been proven a success and Brahms had openly expressed his satisfaction with the result. The sensational outcome could be witnessed in the first concert tour made by the Meiningen musicians to the large cities of northern Germany (during the previous season they had undertaken merely a trial tour, performing in a few cities around Meiningen). Notable were particularly both Brahms concerts in Berlin, on the eighth and ninth of January 1882,[27] where Bülow played the First and Brahms played the Second Piano Concerto while the other conducted the orchestra. (See the commentary to letter no. 3 for the exact stations of that tour.) From that winter on, Bülow's commitment to Brahms became as extensive as imaginable. He even felt responsible, as we know from letter no. 10, for correcting press remarks on Brahms. He also took it upon himself to familiarize the public with Brahms's piano works: As soon as the Meiningen orchestra's concert tour was over, Bülow undertook his annual winter journey to Vienna as a solo pianist, performing on 2 February 1822 his first piano soirée devoted exclusively to Brahms's works (see commentary to letter no. 10).[28] It was a bold venture, and the Viennese papers reported with considerable restraint. Even Eduard Hanslick, otherwise one of the most determined campaigners for Brahms and Bülow in Vienna, found the long evening "quite a strenuous diversion" (*Neue Freie Presse*, 7 February 1882).

The years of mutual effort under the banner of Bülow's Meiningen principles, however, were probably not as free of tension as Bülow's letters suggest. Some of the strain, due in part to differences in character, ensued from personal intercourse. Significantly, most of the "immense tests of patience put to [Brahms] by his hot-headed, passionate, and rash apostle"[29] were noted by Max Kalbeck, himself thin-skinned when it came to Bülow.

Grave indeed, however, was the conflict that evoked the preliminary end of cooperation between Bülow and Brahms. Though it seems insignificant and played up by Bülow, it clearly reveals a problem in Bülow's relationship to Brahms. Thus we must examine it further. It involved for Bülow no less than his own self-esteem as a musician. The utmost concern of their last joint concert trip with the Meiningen orchestra in November 1885 (the itinerary is given in the commentary to letter no. 25) was to present Brahms's Fourth Symphony in large cities along the Rhine and in Holland, where the greater part of the concerts were to be conducted by Brahms. The fact that Brahms had left it up to the Meiningen musicians to present this piece caused a stir in itself, particularly in Frankfurt, the first station on the agenda, where the fourth symphony was considered the most important part of the program. Brahms accompanied Bülow only during certain segments of the tour. He did not think he was doing any harm, then, when—without discussing it with Bülow—he complied to a wish that had been expressed in Frankfurt once before, namely, to allow musicians there to play the symphony at their museum's concert on 5 March the following year. The Meiningen orchestra had already performed the symphony in Frankfurt on the third of November, and it had not been all too well received.[30] It was precisely this halfhearted response to the symphony that at first led Brahms to turn down the request brought forth by the superintendent of the museum and instead, and upon Bülow's urging, to let Bülow have a go at it in his closing concert on 24 November in Frankfurt. But the museum inquired again, and this time Brahms obliged. On the seventeenth of November, Brahms, who had already left town and gone to celebrate the birthday of his friend Rudolph von der Leyen in Krefeld, where he was later to rejoin the conductor and orchestra, wrote to Bülow, informing him of his provisionary consent to the museum's request. The proviso was that Bülow should be given the option to insist on performing the symphony in Frankfurt at his final concert there. Now, in order to understand Bülow's reaction to these events it is important to know that the last concert in Frankfurt was particularly important to him because it was supposed to be the first time during the entire tour that Brahms, who until then had always directed the piece, was to hear the symphony as interpreted and directed by Bülow. Brahms had conducted the first performance of the symphony in Frankfurt, and the very fact that it had been received with reserve made it—so very characteristically—an even greater challenge to Bülow. For Bülow, Brahms's granting the museum permission to play the piece, even though that consent had not been definite, meant betrayal and blatant disesteem. Without replying in writing to Brahms, he simply changed the program of his final concert in Frankfurt, substituting Brahms's Symphony no. 4 with Beethoven's Symphony no. 7. The program had already been printed, so he added a note on the back:

> Out of regard for the revered Museum Society's request to repeat *Johannes Brahms's new (fourth) symphony in E minor* at one of their subscription concerts under the direction of the Master himself, at its second concert the ducal court orchestra shall perform *Beethoven's Symphony No. 7* instead.[31]

Brahms was stunned by Bülow's reaction upon reaching Krefeld. A recently published report sent in December 1885 to the duke in Meiningen is the only account we have of these events in Brahms's own words:[32]

> From the start the plan was that Bülow would present my new symphony *only* at the *first* concert in Frankfurt because the directors of the museum had already once asked me to conduct it for them. To me the project's success then seemed so negligible, that on the road at some point I said to Bülow that the directors would hardly uphold their wish and if he wanted to, he could repeat the symphony at his second concert. When I got to Krefeld I found letters and telegrams asking for permission to use the symphony *if* Bülow were not going to. I sent a telegram to the museum, denying them my consent. But a few days later I wrote to Bülow in Amsterdam, on the side, that I had done something "dumb" and had been unnecessarily inconsiderate toward the Society. Without further ado, Bülow immediately changed the program in question and was so kind as to add "out of regard for the revered directors," etc. I did not expect it of him, otherwise I would have very innocently asked him to do so. I found it particularly friendly and kind of him. Great was my dismay, then, when we met again and I finally discovered how Bülow felt about my letter. I was deeply moved to see him so shocked; as if he had gone through the worst, as if he had seen through to the deepest abyss of a selfish human soul. He had gone through this once with Wagner, he said, and he could not bear it again.

Even before the concert tour ended, on 23 November and writing from Cologne, Bülow sent the duke a petition for release.[33] After the concert in Frankfurt on 24 November he considered his mission over. He left the orchestra to perform one more Brahms concert in Wiesbaden on 25 November under the direction of the composer himself and went back to Meiningen where he was released from his office on the first of December. For the time being, the relation between Bülow and Brahms rested.

It is telling that according to Brahms, Bülow detected an unforeseen and seemingly glaringly exaggerated parallel to the breach of trust by Richard Wagner; he obviously felt deeply injured in the most tender part of his relationship to Brahms. Bülow himself was always creative when it came to capturing the nature of that relationship with novel, equally memorable and yet simplifying metaphors and concepts. His timeworn witticism of Brahms being the "legislative" and he the "executive" half of their relationship can also be found in his correspondence (letter no. 53); he also liked to cite Schiller on the wagoners who always had work because the kings kept building (nos. 24, 35, and 43). Working with Brahms had caused Bülow, who long past his youth ambitiously continued to compose music (although it was never his primary task and was difficult for him), to ultimately accept that his artistic fulfillment lay in reproducing. And yet it often irritated him that Brahms seemed to demonstrate indifference to that work,[34] particularly since the indifference was clearly pretense. When later Brahms (as Ferdinand Schumann says) supposedly spoke against erecting a monument for Bülow in Hamburg on the grounds that a reproductive artist has no right to one,[35] that does thoroughly correspond to his ideal of aesthetics centered on "lasting music":[36] the history of music is the history of masterpieces as described by texts. No doubt, Bülow himself probably saw things in much the same vein and resigned to the distinction in rank. But that everything that highlighted that difference also easily pained him is obvious.[37] Not until later, long after their conflict had been resolved, or perhaps because it had been resolved, did Brahms, in unusual candor, reveal to "our highly desirable Hans von Bülow" why he "couldn't care less about public things" and ask him sincerely to see the other side of Brahms, the side he himself did not like to display. This Brahms told Bülow not coincidentally in a letter reminiscing on the first performance of his Sonata in C major played by the young Bülow (see commentary to letter no. 25). And Brahms never concealed how much he extraordinarily valued Bülow as a pianist (see Brahms's letters from July 1881 and May 1882 and the commentary to Bülow's letters no. 3 and 12).

But how little Brahms actually grasped his friend's sensitivity is evidenced not only by his behavior during the episode of November 1885, but even more so by Brahms's first and unsuccessful attempt at reconciliation in May the following year. Long accustomed to Bülow's irritability, a few days after they went separate ways Brahms did hope "that Hans von Bülow would calm down after quickly recollecting himself, and the brief dissonance would long be canceled and fade away."[38] But that did not happen, and over a year passed before the conflict was finally settled. A letter written by Brahms to Bülow, via the latter's wife, never reached him (see no. 29). Thus Bülow saw his own (meanwhile lost) obligatory birthday greeting for Brahms on 7 May 1886 as the first step toward reestablishing contact. In reply to these greetings, Brahms mentioned his (allegedly detailed) letter from the winter and—lacking any inclination to rehash the embarrassing matter again—sought to play down the events of November 1885 by saying that for him concerts and such "do not count among the most serious things" anyway (see commentary to no. 29). Understandably, this well-meant attempt at appeasement offended Bülow anew, implying as it did that his entire reproductive career was practically worthless. Bülow's petulant and sarcastic reply (no. 29) presents the most conspicuous exception to the otherwise exuberant, sometimes even devoted tone of his letters to Brahms. But then, months later, another of Brahms's initiatives finally restored their old intimacy entirely. In January and February of 1887, Bülow played his round of Beethoven's piano works in four evening concerts (21 and 24 January, and 2 and 7 February) in Vienna. On this occasion, on the first day of his concerts, on the morning of 21 January, at his hotel Bülow received a calling card from Johannes Brahms, on which the latter had written nothing but two and a half measures of notes from the trio in act 2 of the *Magic Flute*: "Shall I, dear, ne'er see thee again?"[39] Bülow, as he wrote to his wife, was instantly solaced and "very touched." "I went to visit him in the afternoon and chatted for a charming hour with this great contemporary. Unfortunately I could not attend Rosa Papier's (sold out) lieder concert with him for fear of the housecat."[40] Brahms and Bülow immediately revived their contact, and for as long as Bülow stayed in Vienna they met every day. Obviously both had long missed their old friendship that was now reestablished. Bülow's participation in an evening concert (performing Brahms's Piano Quintet op. 34) at the Vienna Musician's Association on 2 February even encouraged good-humored Brahms to address the audience "for the first time ever," as Bülow mentions explicitly.[41] Then they "went drinking at a tavern until 2 a.m."[42]

In a wide variety of contexts Bülow said that Brahms meant an "epoch"[43] of his life, one that he characterized, not without coquetry, yet succumbing to his penchant for accuracy, as his "reactionary" phase. "My reactionary disposition waxes. In the years left to me I want to use it to compensate the wrongdoings from the first and second phase of my existence."[44] Within the scope of the present edition of Bülow's letters, it would take us too far to discuss the implications of what it meant in the nineteenth century to be reactionary in terms of music aesthetics, music history, and the philosophy of music. Instead, may I draw the reader's attention to a remarkable theoretical problem alluded to in letters no. 42 and 43 that is particularly interesting because Brahms did not go along with it. Although during his phase of radical "progressiveness" Bülow had removed himself considerably from the views of his former teacher of musical doctrine in Leipzig, Moritz Hauptmann, in his mature years he professed of all things one of the latter's most conservative fundamental axioms. In a standard work on the nature of metrics and harmony, Hauptmann polemically fought enharmonic practices that he considered a widespread trait of contemporary composition technique and that he adamantly dismissed as being "false," careless, and tonality-damaging ways of composing.[45] As a young man, Bülow had mocked "the enemies of enharmonic change,"[46] turning Hauptmann's concepts against him, calling him "a heretic, a teacher of false doctrine."* "If we dismiss enharmonic technique, we're left with reaction, standstill, reversal."[47] Thirty years later he argued the exact opposite—entirely contrary to the reality and musical practices of the late nineteenth century. Upon request he wrote an article for a Hamburg newspaper praising the enharmonium of Japanese physicist Shohé Tanaka as paving the way for the return to "pure" composition, leaving enharmonic and equal temperament behind. In the article, Bülow distorted a Brahms statement that he quoted incorrectly from memory in an attempt to confer validity upon his own position. This induced Brahms to mildly object (see letter no. 48), reversing the quotation to mean almost the opposite, so that it at any rate became quite worthless for Bülow's argument. Overall, Bülow's admiration for Brahms did not mean that their theoretical and aesthetic views coincided. Bülow never shared some of Brahms's values, such as the latter's deep interest in older music (see particularly letter no. 52).

The end of their relationship is puzzling. After the autumn of 1892 Bülow only sporadically enjoyed good health. On 4 October 1892 he gave his last piano soirée in Berlin. He passed the turn of the year, plagued with increasingly intense headaches, in a clinic for nervous disorders near Pankow, staying there until March 1893, when he was once more able to direct orchestral concerts in Berlin and Hamburg. On 10 April 1893 he directed one last concert for the pension fund of the Berlin Philharmonic. Treatments in St. Blasien and Aschaffenburg could not reduce his suffering. Shortly before his sixty-forth birthday he left Hamburg for Egypt, hoping that a climate change might improve his health. On 2 December 1894, Hans von Bülow died in Cairo.

Despite Bülow's chronic ailment, we do not know why their correspondence ebbed after the autumn of 1892. Certainly, a few of the summer's letters had evoked slight discord. Brahms resolutely disapproved of Bülow's plan to erect a monument to Heinrich Heine in Hamburg (see letter 57),[48] and although he eventually did send Bülow some of the new pieces for piano that he had offered, initially he held them back. But save for telegraphically confirming their receipt, Bülow did not otherwise respond, and Brahms, weary of such complications,[49] had to ask Simrock about them. Brahms and Bülow were supposed to meet during Bülow's last piano soirée on 4 October, although the program included neither the originally announced Brahms works nor the compositions that Brahms had just sent in manuscript. But Bülow, exhausted by the performance, was indisposed. Brahms's subsequent

---

*Bülow called Hauptmann an *Irrlehrer*, a pun combining the words *Irrlehre* (heretic doctrine) and *Lehrer* (teacher). CK.

distressed letter to Bülow in October 1892 (see the commentary to no. 57) marks the final document of their correspondence. Their immediate personal contact came to a halt.

Long periods of silence between letters, periods that were interrupted by encounters anyway, were not unusual throughout the entire duration of the Bülow-Brahms correspondence. Yet it is remarkable that the more Brahms heard about Bülow's illness from third parties, the less he was inclined to contact his friend personally. Instead, Brahms used roundabout ways to inquire about Bülow and to send him greetings, most often through the mayor of Hamburg's daughter, Toni Petersen, and later via Bülow's wife. Thus the end of the relationship between Bülow and Brahms is only obliquely reflected in the incomplete historical sources.

A letter from Pankow written by Marie von Bülow on 31 December 1892 and addressed to Toni Petersen is the first sign we have of Brahms's indirect attempt to inquire about Bülow:[50]

> A thousand thanks for being so kind as to report to Brahms. Unfortunately, I find it difficult to feel touched by his belated interest. . . . I have long found it odd that for so many months and among the many inquiries not one was made by the Viennese master. That is, I tried to wonder about it, but actually callousness suits the whole north pole atmosphere of the mind and man spared all neuralgias.

Apparently Toni Petersen replied that Brahms explained his silence by the fact that he had gotten no answer to his letter of October 1892. Marie von Bülow wrote back[51]: "Naturally my husband received Brahms's letter back then, but it called for no immediate reply and for months already my husband had been in no position to write. The silence itself should have puzzled Brahms." Six weeks later, after Toni Petersen reported having personally encountered Brahms in Hamburg and having once again repeated the reason the composer had stated for not writing, Marie von Bülow mentions her own last encounter with Brahms, which took place on 4 October 1892:[52]

> I knew straightaway that your dinner would turn out so nice; I know how very "humane" *gemütlich* Brahms can be. Nonetheless, I am taken aback by his grounds for silence, which I no longer find so "strange." So much talk of that famous letter, as if it had contained world-shaking events or the warmest outpour of friendship! At the time my husband told me nothing of the sort.—We know that Brahms eschews all correspondence; one must have a particular reason for writing to him. . . . During this painful time I myself only wrote to persons of whom I knew that out of deepest sympathy they were "burning" to have news. In Berlin I fervently described

to Brahms how much my husband cherishes any sign of his interest—it embarrasses me now to think that it must have sounded like begging—but I did not want to miss the slightest opportunity to help Hans get what is so important to him, and besides, I was so upset, I had to obey my heart. . . . My mind spins and the day is wholly ruined without my knowing in the least *what* I could possibly write [to Brahms] that would not sound like an accusation or a monition.

Marie von Bülow did write to Brahms, however, and fragments of the letter she sent off the next day still exist, although they have been half-destroyed. Some sections of the beginning and the close of the text are legible:[53]

> Dear Doctor!
> Miss Petersen tells me that your silence during my husband's long, difficult time of illness stems from your not having heard from me *and* uncertainty as to whether your last letter reached us. . . . Since you know my husband's mind, I surely need not assure you that he was pleased to get your lines and that every sign of your concern for him comforts him. . . . I do not know when my husband will once again be able to write.

The letter concludes, as far as can be discerned, with an offer to act as the medium that would uphold contact between Bülow and Brahms. It was, then, the beginning of correspondence between Brahms and Marie von Bülow. One of Brahms's letters from March of the same year became known by being published in the last volume of the collection of Bülow's letters. The occasion was the philharmonic concert of 12 March 1893, directed by Bülow, who seemed to have recovered:[54]

> *Dear Baroness,*
> *like a cheerful telegram, this is meant to reach you tomorrow during the rehearsal, to tell you and your dear esteemed husband that in my thoughts I am there with you and that I have spread the score solemnly before me and am listening more carefully and better than anyone present, while at the same time most pleasurably conversing with you.*
> *I would thank you cordially for your dear letter and tell you that I did not at all expect such a lengthy, detailed reply, just a little echo (a sort of acknowledgment of getting mine), that would enable me to continue corresponding. I had intended, namely, to write something like a journal. If one likes to dance, one will dance in the absence of music.*
> *But I cannot claim that I enjoy writing letters and it takes some prompting. For today I have satisfied that desire and this will not reach you on time during rehearsal, if I do not now quickly repeat my best, most heartfelt greetings as*
> *Your cordially loyal*
> *J. Brahms*

Great relief at word of Bülow's recovery permeates this message and therein perhaps lies an explanation for Brahms's reluctance to write throughout Bülow's illness. How difficult it was for him to express *in words* his grief at the illness and loss of close persons has often been discussed. There is no evidence of any direct contact between Brahms and Bülow after March 1893. But he did apparently take up Marie von Bülow's offer to keep in touch. We know of two letters, both written in August from Ischl. The first, Marie von Bülow revealed to Toni Petersen, "brought my husband to tears."[55] Brahms wrote,[56]

> *Dear and kind Baroness,*
>
> *I deeply, earnestly desire to hear about your dear husband. I desire it twice as much when I see how cordially all of his acquaintances and friends here think of him. I tell myself in vain that you are obliged to write to many and have much to do. I must ask that you send me, too, a word, and I hope for your graciousness. How much more amiable things are, when one knows how he is. And you might, I surely hope, be able to write about more happy prospects!*
>
> *By greeting you and him from my heart I repeat my urgent request for news; you cannot know how gratefully I read every little word.*
>
> *Your deeply and cordially loyal J. Brahms*

The other letter, written on 24 August 1893, replies to news from Marie von Bülow expressing hope that hypnotic treatment might help her husband:

> *Dearest Baroness,*
>
> *I thank you dearly for your letter informing me in such detail of the state of things. If anything is able to alleviate my deeply sad feelings about it, it is your letter itself, so loving and kind and beautiful that it seems to cast a softening veil over everything. Most of all because it reveals how valuable you are to your husband, what he has in you.*
>
> *Give your dear husband my most heartfelt greetings and those of others here, too, particularly from Bösendorfer.*
>
> *Forgive me for denying your request and my own temptation to "speculate" about [the prospects of] your plan! Every second person I talk to most energetically contradicts the first. That would even happen if I were to ask two of the renowned physicians in our area, or even if I myself were to write today and then again tomorrow!*
>
> *May the beautiful Black Forest relieve you of all these complicated worries—or may the magician in Nancy be as good at his trade as his patient is with an entire orchestra!*
>
> *Cordially wishing the best, your very loyal*
> *J. Brahms*

This message is the last known. Brahms heard of Bülow's death from Toni Petersen. He expressed his sympathy in his own indirect way by asking her[57] to convey his condolences to Bülow's widow and his publisher and trustee Simrock to transfer one thousand marks each to the pension funds of both orchestras that Bülow had conducted. It was to be done the day of the funeral, and only Bülow's widow was to learn the name of the donor. Brahms, who lost several friends that spring, including Theodore Billroth and Philipp Spitta, was deeply shaken by Bülow's death. He himself, who until then had hardly ever been seriously ill, survived Bülow by only three years.

NOTES

1. La Mara (Marie Lipsius), ed., *Hans von Bülow: Briefwechsel mit Franz Liszt* (Leipzig, 1898), p. 43. "Whether Mozart-Brahms or Schumann-Brahms, the matter definitely does not disturb my sleep. I'll wait and see what happens."

2. BBS III/1, p. 137.

3. BBS II (2), p. 162 (letter dated 1 January 1854).

4. La Mara, *Hans von Bülow: Briefwechsel mit Franz Liszt*, p. 61.

At Joachim's home you will meet Brahms whom I sincerely find interesting and who behaved with tact and good taste toward me throughout a few days that I just spent in Leipzig in honor of Berlioz. Also, I invited him several times for dinner and it pleases me in hindsight to believe that his "New Paths" converge much more with Weimar. You will like his Sonata op. 1, that I went through the proof sheets of in Leipzig and that he had already shown to me here. It is exactly the kind of work that has given me a better idea of his talent at composing.

5. BBS II (2), p. 166.

6. Marie von Bülow, *Hans von Bülow. Ausgewählte Briefe* [Selected Letters], popular ed. (Leipzig, 1919), p. 102f.; letter to Julius Schaeffer dated 10 January 1854.

7. See a letter dated 7 March 1854, shortly after Schumann's admittance to a sanatorium: "I had so much looked forward to coming closer to this rare, great artistic mind, an encounter that recently Joachim had so eagerly prepared that at his request Robert Schumann asked me to come visit him sometime" (BBS II [2], p. 187).

8. See BBS II (2), p. 303, dated 8 December 1854.

9. It did not, however, terminate the relationship; when a year earlier Joachim Raff had separated from Liszt it did not seriously endanger his friendship with Bülow either (cf. BBS IV [3], p. 83).

10. BBS IV (3), p. 135, dated 28 November 1857.

11. BBS IV (3), p. 551, dated 22 October 1863.

12. BBS IV (3), p. 49.

13. BBS III/1, p. 318 (reviewed in January 1858).

14. See BBW V, p. 274.

15. Letter to Louis Köhler dated 12 May 1860 (BBS IV [3], p. 317). The names were rendered illegible by the editor, but it is known that they included Robert

Radecke, Konstantin Vierling, and others not identified (SBB, Sign.: Mus. ep. Hans von Bülow 393).

16. Bülow writes of "mobs" and "idiots" in the letter to Louis Köhler mentioned in note 15 above. In a letter to Hans von Bronsart (dated 10 October 1861), he writes, "Regarding Brahms and his accomplices, I cannot fathom your esteem for them. My motto for that scoundrel is Tannhäuser's* "Thee seek I not, nor thine!" May they, in their low introverting instinct, sail to the harbor of Bonn's recluse sanatorium. Either Liszt's music is nonmusic, or these people are off track. There is no way in between or 'Langegasse' [long lane, i.e. long way] as they say" (printed with omissions in BBS IV [3], p. 440; the original can be found in SBB, Sign.: Mus. ep. Hans von Bülow 43). "Langegasse" alludes to Franz Brendel's address in Leipzig. Brendel revised the *New Journal for Music* and founded in 1861 the *Allgemeiner Deutscher Musikverein* (General German Music Association) and—contrary to Bülow—tried to mediate between the parties.

17. BBS IV (3), p. 604, dated 29 September 1864.

18. BBS V (4), p. 158, letter to Joachim Raff dated 22 November 1866.

19. As in Berlin on 19 February 1873 where a note added to Scherzo I reads, "from [Schumann's] papers edited by Joh. Brahms" (printed program among Bülow's papers in SBB, Sign.: Db 1815 [2]).

20. BBS VI (5), p. 443.

21. BBS VI (5), p. 444.

22. Not on 26 April 1878, as stated mistakenly in Kalbeck 3/2, p. 232. At this concert Joachim played the solo Violin Concerto op. 11 and Schubert's Violin Fantasy in C major accompanied by Bülow at the piano.

23. Kalbeck 3/2, p. 306.

24. See Alfred Erck, Inge Erck, and Herta Müller, *Hans von Bülows Meiniger Jahre,* in *Südthüringer Forschungen* 25 (Beiträge zur Musikgeschichte Meiningens) [South Thuringia Research 25 (Essays on Music History at Meiningen)] (Meiningen, 1990), p. 23.

25. Found together with Hiller's reply in Reinhold Sietz, ed., *Aus Ferdinand Hillers Briefwechsel* [Ferdinand Hiller's Correspondence], vol. 4 (Cologne, 1964), p. 174f.

26. Letter to Hermann Wolff dated 27 October 1881, BBS VII [6], p. 100f.

27. Cf. Florence May's detailed report on the concert of 8 January and the morning rehearsal. Florence May, *The Life of Johannes Brahms*, vol. 1 (London, 1905), p. 26f.

28. In a letter to Simrock dated 3 February 1882, Bülow relates a pleasant event that happened at this concert: "It was a felicitous evening. Just as last year Brahms had listened to my Liszt concert with kind appreciation, this time Liszt (traveling from Venice to Budapest) heard me play Brahms's works. Liszt, known for falling asleep at every concert, had intent eyes and ears yesterday. This led—thank heavens—to a very friendly encounter backstage during the break" (BBS VII [6], p. 143).

---

* *Nicht such ich Dich, noch Deiner Sippschaft einen.* Upon return from his pilgrimage to Rome, Tannhäuser says that he wants nothing to do with Wolfram or any of the other knightly minnesingers (Walter von der Vogelweide, Biterolf, Heinrich the Scribe, or Reinmar von Zweter) who had expulsed him from their midst due to his unbridled eroticism. The remark is an insult to Brahms and the other musicians. CK

29. Kalbeck 3/2, p. 489.

30. The concert review in the *Frankfurter Zeitung* dated 4 November 1885: "After hearing it *once* we believe it can be said with a fair amount of certainty that following his highly significant 'Third' [symphony], Brahms's 'Fourth' can hardly be called *progress*."

31. Printed program among Bülow's papers (SBB, Sign.: Db 1815 [5]).

32. BBW XVII, p. 63.

33. This petition for release was merely the last of many (he wrote the first on 8 April 1884) and does not mention the true reason but contains instead the characteristic Bülow twist that he does not feel "enough like a court counselor to continue cranking the Beethoven-Brahms hurdy-gurdy endlessly." Indeed, "during the last three weeks it was only by making use of artificial stimulants and sometimes by the presence of Master Brahms that I was able to suppress nausea at the habitual trade-likeness of this business that draws us to the demoralizing offensive cliffs of humbug, grandstanding, and plaudit wooing" (quoted from Erck, Erck, and Müller [see note 24], p. 49).

34. See a report by Richard Strauss, who had just arrived in Meiningen and who experienced the rehearsal of Symphony no. 4. Richard Strauss, *Betrachtungen und Erinnerungen*, ed. Willi Schuh (Munich, 1989), p. 206.f; *Recollections and Reflections* (London, 1953).

35. Ferdinand Schumann, *Erinnerungen an Johannes Brahms* [Remembering Johannes Brahms], in *Neue Zeitung für Musik* (1915), p. 228.

36. See Gustav Jenner, *Johannes Brahms als Mensch, Lehrer und Künstler* [Johannes Brahms: The Person, Teacher and Artist] (Marburg, 1905), p. 74.

37. Regarding Bülow's composing, there do exist written comments by his early mentors Liszt and Wagner, but none by Brahms. Brahms's musical papers contain only a single piece composed by Bülow: the score for four character pieces, op. 23. Brahms's estate also contains the first two volumes of Bülow letters edited by his widow, both of which had been published prior to Brahms's death (cf. Hofmann, p. 149).

38. BBW XVII, p. 60 (letter to George II dated 30 November 1885).

39. BBS VII (7), p. 73, footnote 1.

40. The original is in SBB, Sign.: Mus. ep. Hans von Bülow 1119. The episode can also be found in BBS VIII (7), p. 73, where the allusion to Marie von Bülow's notorious jealousy has been omitted.

41. BBS VIII (7), p. 76.

42. BBS VIII (7), p. 76.

43. BBS VII (6), p. 176, letter to Marie Schanzer dated 23 May 1882.

44. BBS VIII (7), p. 44, letter to Hermann Wolff dated 18 July 1886.

45. Moritz Hauptmann, *Die Natur der Harmonik und der Metrik* (Leipzig, 1853), p. 189.

46. BBS II (2), p. 216, letter to Franz Liszt dated 29 June 1854, written in French.

47. BBS IV (3), p. 325, in a letter to Louis Köhler dated 26 June 1860.

48. To Simrock, Brahms spoke abrasively of Bülow's suggestion: "One cannot seriously discuss Bülow's notions" (BBW XII, p. 75, dated 26 September 1892).

49. BBW XII, p. 75, dated 26 September 1892.

50. Copy (by Marie von Bülow herself) in SBB, Sign.: NL Hans von Bülow D IV, 66.

51. From Pankow, dated 3 January 1893; in SBB, Sign.: NL Hans von Bülow D IV, 66.

52. Letter to Toni Petersen, also written from Pankow, dated 14 February 1893; in SBB, Sig. NL Hans von Bülow D IV, 66.

53. Vienna City and National Library [Wiener Stadt- und Landesbibliothek]; Manuscripts, Sign.: I. N. 165.300.

54. BBS VIII (7), p. 419.

55. BBS VIII (7), p. 447.

56. BBS VIII (7), p. 447.

57. See Kurt Hofmann, *Brahmsiana der Familie Petersen: Erinnerungen und Briefe*, in *Brahms Studies* 3 (Hamburg, 1979), p. 102f.

Abbreviations

BBS: Marie von Bülow, ed., *Hans von Bülow: Briefe und Schriften*, 8 vols. (Leipzig, 1895–1908). Volumes I and II and volumes IV to VIII contain the letters; volume III is comprised of two half volumes containing other writings (quotations are from the 1911 enhanced edition). For the sake of clarity, roman numerals indicate the volume number from the complete edition, while the number in parentheses indicates the volume of letters. Thus BBS IV (3) means *Briefe und Schriften*, vol. IV (third volume of letters); BBS III/2 means *Briefe und Schriften*, second half of vol. III.

BBW: *Johannes Brahms Briefwechsel* (Johannes Brahms Correspondence), edited and published in several volumes by the German Brahms Society, Berlin, beginning in 1906. (The entire set of volumes was reprinted in Tutzing in 1974.) Beginning with volume XVII, I have used the new series, *Johannes Brahms Briefwechsel Neue Folge*, published in Tutzing in 1991.

Geiringer: Karl Geiringer, *Brahms: Sein Leben und Schaffen*, 2nd printing (Zurich, 1995).

Hofmann: Kurt Hoffmann, *Die Bibliothek von Johannes Brahms: Bücher- und Musikalienverzeichnis* [The Library of Johannes Brahms: Index of Books and Music Items] (Hamburg, 1974).

Kalbeck: Max Kalbeck, *Johannes Brahms*, 4 vols. (each with two parts), published in Berlin beginning in 1904. Quotations are from the most recent reprint edition, Tutzing, 1976.

SBB: *Staatsbibliothek Berlin* (National Library at Berlin, Prussian Cultural Heritage Foundation, Department of Music).

Letters and Commentary

LETTERS

No. 1

[2 October 1877]

Hanover, 2 Oct. 1877

Rudolph's Hotel

Distinguished Master!

Might you kindly ask Massa Simrock[1] on behalf of the director and interim conductor at Welfenheim[2] for permission to perform "the tenth"[3] symphony on the twentieth [of this month] at our third subscription concert? Naturally the publisher shall be properly compensated for we shall later purchase all the printed parts for an inevitable repeat performance. But since it is taking so terribly long to get them printed, would it not be possible to get permission to perform the piece in the meantime using handwritten parts? Perhaps borrowed from Karlsruhe?[4]

Please help! Simrock did not answer Mr. Von Bronsart's recent letter.[5]

In reverent admiration,

Your Hans von Bülow

Urgent

Letter No. 1. *Staatsbibliothek zu Berlin—Preussischer Kulturbesitz; SBB Mus. Ep. Hans von Bülow 281*

No. 2

[15 October 1877]

Hanover, 15 Oct. 1877

Distinguished Master,

Simrock's incredibly rude behavior toward Mr. Von Bronsart, his more than inconsiderate neglect to finally answer with a (prepaid[1]) yes or no my request regarding whether we may rehearse your symphony tomorrow, and so on, has just inspired me to send a telegram as worded below, of which I have also of course informed others.

"I must note something else that Beethoven and Brahms have in common: uncouth publishers."

HvB[2]

Please don't be angry with me—I'm furious that I cannot present your symphony on the twentieth[3] before I leave![4]

Thank you for your recent kind letter. Esteemed greetings from your total and partial admirer

Hans v. Bülow

No. 3

[15 August 1881]

Meiningen, 15 August 1881
(Saxon Court)[1]

Most distinguished Master!

Not until returning yesterday from travel that did not restore my health did I receive your letter from last month.[2] Thank you for remembering my offer; by accepting it you would honor us at any time. *At any time*, that it, that I have the ducal orchestra at my disposal. That is unfortunately only part of the year. The musicians are paid so poorly that they must be allowed to work on the side at bath resorts during the summer to avert the curse of their future widows and orphans.

The musicians are all back on October 3, however, and could work with you every morning until year's end, for whatever experiment you have in mind. It would be nice, of course, if you could give us two weeks to musically spruce ourselves up a bit. That would be good not only for long-standing players, but for the string quartet backup as well, that I cannot get until late September. Let's say, then: We could begin in *mid-October*.

That would give me an opportunity to first thoroughly rehearse both of your symphonies so that you could evaluate and correct our interpretation. Your advice is all the more important to me because then when the court orchestra begins its concert tour after New Years we could, at least in larger cities

(Leipzig and Berlin),[3] add 2 or 3 Brahms soirées to our specialty of Beethoven concerts. May I later consult you on the order of programs for those soirées?

With most cordial wishes for your well-being, I remain in sincere admiration and adoration,

Your wholly subservient Hans v. Bülow

No. 4

[13 September 1881]

Meiningen, 13 Sept. 1881

Most distinguished Sir and Master!

Beginning on Monday, Oct. 17, the ducal court orchestra that practices during the first months of winter every morning and afternoon (except Sundays) under my direction will be at your disposal, whenever you wish, for trying out your new piano concerto. We will all do our utmost to deserve the honor you bestow on us by letting us participate in this experiment. The wind section should satisfy you entirely; regarding the string quartet I beg for lenience: due to repeated replacements, the ensemble will need weeks of continued practice to attain the desired standard. Perhaps you can do us the favor of adopting our method: first sight-read together, then practice the parts of the accompaniment separately (winds alone, strings alone), and then add the principal part.

The Bechstein grand piano is no longer quite new, but still suitable (comfortable to play, with a noble sound) and will certainly not out of pride at being without equal in this small town resist finding a *modus ludendi*.

Enclosed is the program[1] for our local concert season—short, but "dense" (at Christmas we leave the stage to the theater)—to give you an idea of how things "look" here.

In terms of exploring the natural beauty of Thuringia, there is no one less knowledgeable and thus more inappropriate as a guide or advisor than

Your in sincere admiration entirely subservient
Hans von Bülow

No. 5

[11 October 1881]

Meiningen, 11 Oct. 81
4 Charlotte Street

Most admired Master!

Since I have taken up private accommodations yesterday it will not be difficult for me to reserve for you the rooms I have vacated at Hotel Saxon

Court. I shall have a cottage piano (*pianino*) brought there for you, the "best" one I can find in this royal residence village (of 10,000 inhabitants, including the military). Now I do ask that you pack your bag with a considerable supply of goodwill and lenity, for I have had considerable misfortune with my musicians. The extras (including the second oboe, second flute, third horn and diverse strings) are not too bright, rather matching the dull compensation offered them. In addition, several cases of illness have hampered the first rehearsals, of which that of *both contrabasses* is particularly annoying because the one E-string player is also our bass trombonist. That won't disturb your new piano concerto, but it does change the symphonies that I intend to perform for you. Would you be inclined, despite these possible deficiencies (perhaps happy news of your arrival will elicit a medical miracle) to hear your works anyway? I would also ask you to help us perfect the serenade in A major.

The honor you bestow on us has already aroused envy, which must have caused the note I just discovered in the *Berliner Tageblatt*[1] and that I will correct immediately in an appropriate way (though I wonder how the matter became public). It says (just as perfidious as it is ridiculous) that you are coming here "to study your piano concerto with me." I shall simply retort that you are coming here to correct our studies of your symphonic works.[2] That, I believe, puts things in the right perspective.

Most grateful in advance, your most sincere admirer,

Hans v Bülow

On which train will you arrive?

No. 6

[13 October 1881]

Meiningen, 13 Oct. 1881

Most Distinguished Master!

His Highness the Duke,[1] presently residing (as he usually does in October) at a little hunting pavilion in Kissel near Liebenstein, would be very pleased to meet you.

I am to report to him whether you will be arriving Monday morning or afternoon. It looks as if he will arrange his return to Meiningen accordingly and then spend a few days here.

You will find pleasant rooms and tolerable food at the Hotel Saxon Court and a new, but rather plebian *pianino*. Please do me the most sincere favor of being my guest there.

The wind parts for your second piano concerto and for Schiller's "Nänie" [elegy],[2] arrived yesterday from Vienna.

Would it be a great sacrifice for you to also rehearse your first concerto with us once to show us how it goes? Daring to hope that you will, I am presently preparing it. Regarding the second [concerto] I can only give the winds their parts and tell them to find their way through it because the most important tool for a preliminary rehearsal is still missing, namely, the conductor's score.[3]

As a matter of principle I must confess that I violated my own principles by replying to the attached telegram from Marseille[4] that the newspaper announcement was contrived. We don't need an audience at our rehearsals; the Duke himself will be so discreet as to join us only when you agree to it. I heard that once in Basel (1867) you sent your landlady to her private chamber because she played your unfinished requiem to music director Walter.[5]

For the requiem the first group rehearsal for men and women will take place on Monday evening, which I implore you *not* to attend. I don't recall whether I told you that it was just a year ago September that Mr. Hilpert,[6] at my suggestion, founded the choir club. To want to perform your requiem after thirteen months of frequently interrupted practice is impudence that only a small town resident would condone. Which doesn't mean that it might not turn out well anyway. The performance is planned for 20 November,[7] and we will practice four times a week.

Forgive my idle chatter, the result of bustle and haste. See you soon.

Your most obedient, subservient

H v Bülow

No. 7

[25 October 1881[1]]

Meiningen, the evening of Oct. 25

Distinguished Master,

the honor of having you work with us is worth a little extra trouble. Therefore I do accept your suggestion to have the Brahms concert on November 27, instead of December 11.

1) Tragic Overture, 2) New Piano Concerto, 3) Haydn Variations, 4) Symphony in C minor—the latter hopefully under your "personal" direction.[2] Do you agree?

Excuse the brevity, unfortunately I am yet in such poor health that I must lie down again.

Your most sincere admirer,

H v Bülow

Maar. 25 Oct.
Abend.

Hochverehrter Meister,

die über Ihre Mitwirkung ist schon verschieden...
Arrangements unsererseits ... Ich
acceptire also den von Ihnen vorgeschlagenen
27 Nov. statt des 11 Dez. für das Brahms-
Concert.
1) Trag. Ouv. 2) Nänie Chorus compos
3) Hydn variationen 4) C moll Symphonie –
letztere geschaut unter Ihrer "persönl." Direktion.
Passt es Ihnen so? —
In großer Eile – leider in noch so schwachem
Gesundheitszustand, daß ich mich wieder in
die horizontale Lage begeben muß.

Ihr aufrichtigster bewundernder

H v Bülow

Letter No. 7. *Staatsbibliothek zu Berlin— Preussischer Kulturbesitz; SBB Mus. Ep. Hans von Bülow 287*

No. 8

[28 October 1881]

Meiningen, Oct. 28

Most Honored Master!

After receiving your postcard I immediately summoned chamber musician Abbass[1] (responsible for our music library) and he assures me that the or-
ders you gave to our orchestra attendant[2] to forward the music sheets to your
publisher in Berlin were followed correctly, but that some postal formalities,
such as duty declarations, caused a slight delay. By now the papers "should"
have arrived at their destination. I hope so: Please don't blame me, I knew
nothing about it.

Enclosed are some letters for you that were given to me, apparently they
were sent to the hotel.

Your wholly subservient admirer,
H v Bw

No. 9

[16 November 1881]

Meiningen, 16 Nov.

Most Distinguished Master!

It is fine that you will keep your word. The Duke shall invite the Distinguished, as befits his rank, to reside in the palace, in other words, at the *more
real* "Saxon Court." I assume you have already received the telegram.[1] Now,
a word about the program.

It will not suit "our" audience well to follow the *Gaudeamus* [fun] with
the first movement of the Symphony in C minor. Please don't be frustrated
that I am placing the Academic Festival Overture behind the symphony after
all.[2]

The first half of the concert thus begins with the Tragic Overture, then
the concerto in B major, and finally the Saint Anthony Variations to give you
time to relax your hands. The second half begins with the symphony in C
minor, followed by the Academic Festival Overture. It, too, begins in a minor
key and thus contrasts with the end of the symphony.

The Requiem, which we have been rehearsing diligently, will be not only
presentable, but actually quite presentable. Forgive me this bit of boasting.

Your subservient (still ill and lacking a contrabass*) admirer,
H v Bülow

No. 10

[25 January 1882]

Meiningen-Deiningen*

25 January 82

Esteemed Master!

Dear Friend!¹**

   How are you? Will I perhaps meet you in Vienna, whereto I shall steam***
this week to give a Brahms soirée debut?¹ (Just for Kalbeck,² of course.)

   May I tell you the news? On the twentieth we took Leipzig by storm.³
In mid-March I shall lay the keys and 𝄞 of the conquered city at your feet,
or hand them over to Sim[rock] if you are not around. I doubt that your
publisher has worries: He has been compensated by His Excellence Koch⁴ for
lending you his second syllable.

   In the most recent number of the *Deutsche Musikzeitung*,⁵ Lessmann⁶
revoked what they had written in Hamburg about your talent at the piano.⁷
But the brashest, although it shall not long remain unexemplarily unpunished,
were the *Signals* about the New Year's concert!⁸

   Don't be cross at me, dear *Compthur*⁹ bearer and composer, for writing of
such bagatelles. I feel somewhat light-headed and must first laboriously digest
my "successes" like a boa constrictor.

   *Could you possibly come to Leipzig in mid-March to direct op. 15 for me, and
whatever else you like?* The program will be the same as on 15 January in Ham-
burg.¹⁰

   Recently our dedi-kitten of op. 79¹¹ listened so endearingly: I glanced at
her often and thought of you and suddenly things went so briskly and nicely.
Res severa . . . etc.¹²

   His Highness our duke has had your photograph adeptly enlarged to life
size by someone from Stuttgart. I have not seen it yet, I've only heard that
it's fabulous.

   That's it.—If you can (when in Schiedam¹³), send me a friendly word
at the Bösendorfer address. Most loyally, the one you rescued from Wotan &
Co.-Sansara,

Knipperdolling junior, called Bülow¹⁴

No. 11

[Telegram, Christiania,¹ 7 May 1882]

   Wishes of safety and happiness for the beloved distinguished master from
his most loyal admirer = Bülow.

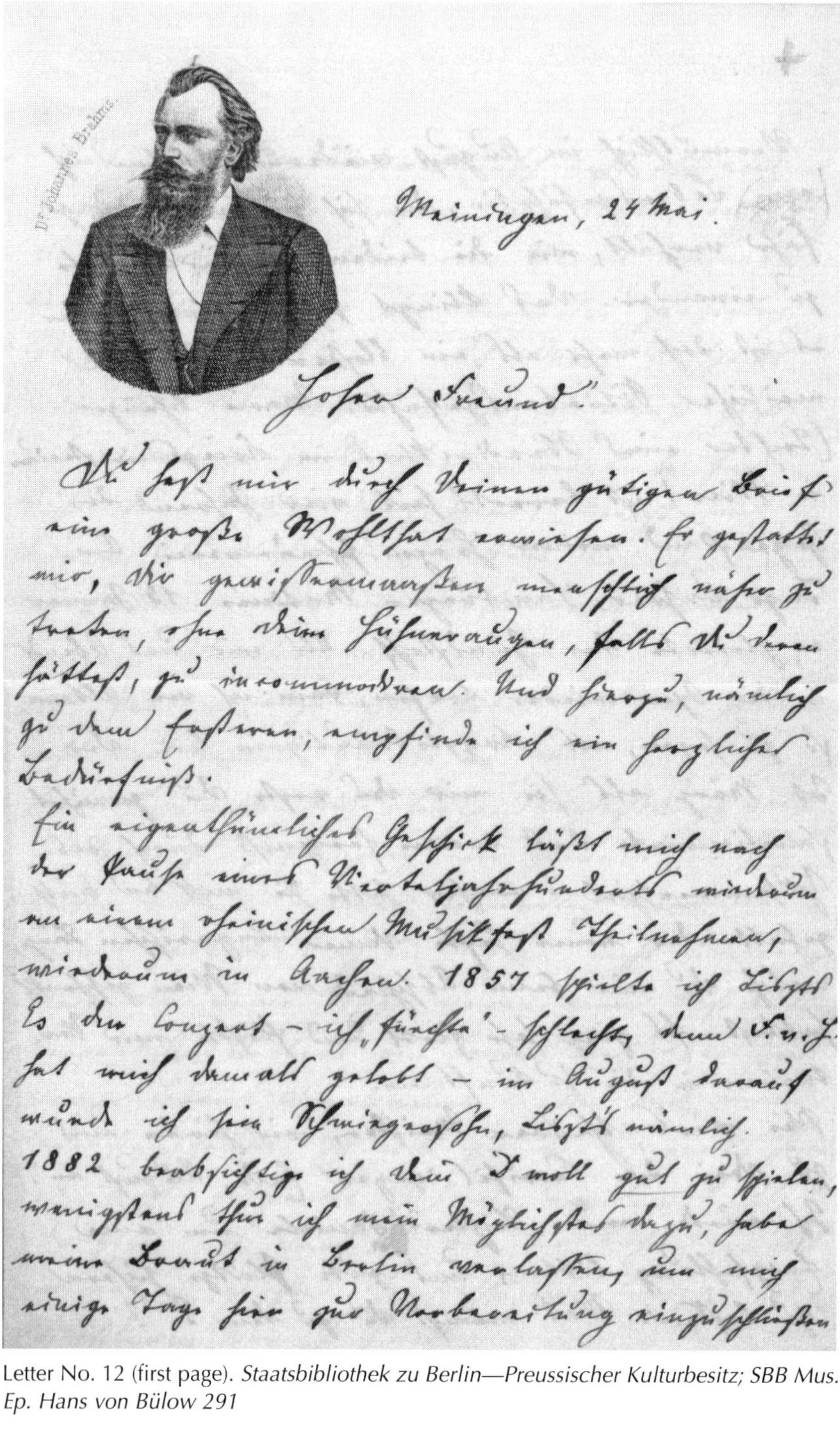
Dr. Johannes Brahms.

Meiningen, 24 Mai.

Hehrer Freund!

Du hast mir durch Deinen gütigen Brief eine grosse Wohlthat erwiesen. Er gestattet mir, Dir gewissermassen menschlich näher zu treten, ohne deine Hühneraugen, falls Du deren hättest, zu incommodieren. Und hierzu, nämlich zu dem Letzteren, empfinde ich ein herzliches Bedürfniss.

Ein eigenthümliches Geschick lässt mich nach der Pause eines Vierteljahrhunderts wiederum an einem rheinischen Musikfest Theilnehmen, wiederum in Aachen. 1857 spielte ich Liszts Es dur Concert – ich fürchte – schlecht, denn F. u. J. hat mich damals gelobt – im August darauf wurde ich sein Schwiegersohn, Liszt's nämlich.

1882 beabsichtige ich den D moll gut zu spielen, wenigstens thu ich mein Möglichstes dazu, habe meine Braut in Berlin verlassen um mich einige Tage hier zur Vorbereitung einzuschliessen

Letter No. 12 (first page). *Staatsbibliothek zu Berlin—Preussischer Kulturbesitz; SBB Mus. Ep. Hans von Bülow 291*

No. 12

[24 May 1882]

Meiningen, 24 May

Esteemed Friend!

Your kind letter has been a great comfort to me. It allows me to approach you personally, without stepping on your toes.[1] And my desire to do so is heartfelt.

Peculiar luck has brought it about that after a pause of a quarter of a century I am once more to participate in a Rhine music festival, and once again in Aachen.[2] In 1857 I performed Liszt's E-flat major, poorly, I'm afraid, because back then F. v. H.[3] praised me—and the following August I became Liszt's son-in-law. Now, in 1882 I plan to play your D minor *well*, or at least do my best, and I have left my bride in Berlin to have a few days of seclusion here to prepare. I shall probably once again marry in August, this time a woman that is to the first as the two piano concertos are to one another. That sounds quite pathetic, but it is meant to more than merely echo [the month of] May's sentiments. Marie Schanzer[4] (daughter of a director at the Vienna department of defense) has captivated my heart for about four years. At our matinee in Hamburg on January 15[5] it burst into flame. When we met again at the opera in the evening (I had come from Altona), I arrived, as it were, a crypto-groom. March 30th sanctioned these intimate events when she allowed me to personally address her with "*Du*" and for the first time—as she lacked the courage beforehand—we together played the new booklets of your Hungarian Dances that you had given me when I left Vienna. It went briskly and gave me confidence in the future.

How about the three of us going to hear *Parsifal* at the end of August? I could ask my daughter Daniela[6] to reserve good seats for us. How about the ?

But, please do not feel inconvenienced by this wish. The role that you play in the final third or fourth of my life should impose no personal representational costs on you. My respect for you, you do know this, is just as great as my deep esteem and love for you. In this respect, the neophyte may audaciously compete with your luckier oldest friend J. J.,[7] even in grasping your entire worth, for which I still owe you proof. But believe me, it will come.

Please don't smile disapprovingly at my pouring out my heart, it takes effort to put it in so few words. Think kindly of me, when you think of me: I'm not worthy of it. Don't worry about your absence at Lake Como[8] being misinterpreted, but do send my bride your new lieder with a penned greeting. For the sake of Simrock, I do not want you to "give" them to me. Miss Schanzer, by the way, will remain Mrs. Schanzer for the stage: she has truly great acting talent, she is an artist from G. G.

She will be performing from 1 June to 15 July in Nuremberg, where I will visit her if it doesn't collide with my other duties, such as visiting my poor blind mother,[9] who is aging with the century.

Good-bye, approve of my most cordial wish to fulfill all of your wishes,

Your very personal admirer,

Hans v. Bülow

I shall greet Wüllner in Aachen[10] from you; he is most indebted to you for your sympathy with the tragic outcome of "his *liaison* with the theater."[11]

No. 13

[23 June 1882]

Meiningen, 23 June 82

My esteemed Friend!

Infandum dolorem renovasti.[1] That is all the worse, because you, and you only, are responsible for your co-republican E. K.[2] catching me off guard. When I visited the arcades or colonnades the second time, I went up to him, as you had done in January. He did not let me go until I appreciated everything worthy of merit that he had to say about his work, the galley proofs spread out on the piano rack. And then he wanted me to put the oral niceties in writing. What will a prisoner not do to seize and regain his freedom—flatter and feign! But that I should have E. K.'s *indispensable du pianiste*[3] in my own home, well, that's almost slander. If there were anything to it, I naturally would not hesitate, to satisfy by express mail your longing based on

Letter No. 13, second page. *Staatsbibliothek zu Berlin—Preussischer Kulturbesitz; SBB Mus. Ep. Hans von Bülow 292*

I'm very glad that you found my recent giddy suggestion impractical, namely, to join me on a pilgrimage to *Parsifal*.[5] I feel just the same. Is it because of the false Demetrius arrangement[6] (probably not) or my antitoxicological musical mood . . . enough, I shall forbear participating in that stage-consecrating festival just as enthusiastically as I now, here, in total solitude, devote myself to the study of your second concerto and with which I shall be so impertinent as to threaten to compete with you next season.

For today I am putting off writing of other personal matters that would call for slight congratulations.

You're probably no longer interested in stale greetings from the director[7] of the 59th Lower Rhine Music Festival, who recently asked me to convey them to you. Be so kind as to accept mine, that are fresher, and, although I cannot fulfill your frantic wish, think well of your loyal warm admirer,

Hans v Bülow

No. 14

[17 July 1882]

Meiningen, 17 July 82

My highly esteemed Friend!

His Excellence Simrock just gave me a wonderful present; but I believe *You* are the one to whom I owe my deepest gratitude. I am very proud to own an *Ex. avant la lettre* score of your concerto in B major,[1] which my fingers had already memorized (as far as possible after seeing it once), even before I held the score in my hands. I can hardly say how happy it has made me and how I felt awe repeatedly throughout the piece. Your music heals my body and soul. Both, as you know, need cleansing of toxins. Well, my ex-idols make that easy enough; Weimar[2] is nonsense, Bayreuth[3] is madness, the first has method, the second a lack of it, but both are a negation of what can be called music! My god, to think *that's where I've been!* May I congratulate you on moving up? The newest Bavarian encyclical[4] calls you *Euripides* (Bach being Aeschylus, Beethoven Sophocles), prophesying that only two of Beethoven's symphonies will endure, whereas nine of yours will. May the latter be true.[5] *Quod Dî bene vertant!*

I have the greatest respect for your songs.[6] How much art*work* is hidden in your art! I listen and look at it all through a magnifying glass and as long as I analyze it, I can't get to the pleasure, to being gripped and moved. For someone like me, the latter is the *ultimate* goal. I cannot let my pure musical interest be forced to cede to charming surprises, if I want to achieve an intuitive emotional effect. Thus my admiration for your newest work is still cold as it were. Is it just my imagination, or are you now really taking a different path, or perhaps an old one? Alas, the title is revealing. These are just *lieder*, not so-called songs, as I thoughtlessly called them above. The poor Franzians,[7] when they realize what candle you have lit! It reminds me of what R. Sch.[8] said when David[9] once played Mendelssohn in Leipzig: well, now you're playing the piece that you always promised us to compose. What a lovely piano arrangement, by the way! Don't laugh, just think of how difficult these tasks are for me—considering my exiguous tools![10] I'm currently practicing op. 1 & 5 as strappingly as possible. Though *you* don't care for your first works any longer, at least don't spoil my desire for them. I want to, and I shall play them so beautifully that you will hark without displeasure at them wafting from Bösendorfer's courtyard. With that challenge in mind, I close this greeting that you don't really need, but that I hope you won't mind,

Your, in deep admiration most loyal
Hans v Bülow

I and R's widow in Fr.[11] were pleased by your warm condolences, for it matches my admiration of your magnanimity to know that the callousness others have contrived regarding this and that is untrue.

No. 15

[7 January 1883]

Distinguished Master and kind Friend!

Momentarily I feel quite unworthy of your written fanfare. The evil spirits—if I may give revolting mobs of nerves such a genteel name—in my most noble part, my head, have been called to order at least a little by electric treatment. But they continue to cause trouble in my fingers, such that I can neither dabble at the piano nor write very well. Recalling my past, happier birthday, today I tried to play your C-major trio (Allah il Allah!), but it brought me extreme dissatisfaction with my own ability. Luckily you don't use the telephone to call me at Meiningen.

But since it would be a *crimen laesae* to postpone answering your inquiry, I have written to His Highness about your wish to come here in early February (instead of early April); I did not give him your letter, though. I have just received the duke's reply:

"Since Maestro Brahms wants to come to the Sicilian bandits* in somewhat barren Girgenti, he is welcome in early February and will naturally be my guest, which you will be so kind as to arrange. But for now, we must shake up our choir and get them in shape for the *Parzenlied*."

[At the bottom of the duke's stationery:] "*But if they attack you, I will demand ransom from the Bayreuth patronage club."

Is that fine with you? Do you want to hear *Nänie* and the D-major ser-enade? The quintet is being rehearsed diligently. To top it off, the princess [1] will play four-handed with the conductor. How about doing it together?

Allow me also to express my deepest gratitude that you have given me your new works, sent to me by your publisher. It's actually unworthy of me and him because it reduces my value as a buyer of your works—and other values as well. To spend money on good music is the only real monetary pleasure.

Good-bye, great one, and please be patient with these hurried and invol-untarily illegible return greetings from

Your loyal admirer,
H v Bw
Meiningen Train Station [2]
7. Jan. 83

No. 16

[10 December 1883]
Superintendent of the Ducal Court Orchestra

Meiningen, 10 Dec. 1883

Noble Master,
Dear Friend,

cordial thanks for your kind return greeting! And thank you for the kind attention given my wife in Vienna!

I read Kalbeck, [1] Hanslick, [2] and Galle-Spei-del. [3] If you have extra copies of the first two, please circulate them among the members of the orchestra.

On January 6th we will begin a tour of southern Germany, returning around the 24th. In February we'll tour the north for two weeks, perform-ing mostly in the free cities, that—thanks to your support in Hamburg—have remained so well-disposed toward us. In March I will give a few solo concerts in Holland and other places to straighten out my finances that due to my inca-pacity last year are in such disarray. But "most naturally" I will try to arrange things such that I am back where I belong when and if you decide to honor our "freight train station" again by paying us a visit. Last Friday in Wiesbaden Madame Henriette [4] told me most pleasantly of the events in Vienna on De-cember 2nd. She would also like to hear us play some of your works here soon (I have finally gotten No. 2, thank you!). Please be so kind as to send the duke, his daughter, or wife, a few words of introduction for our lady friend so that they will treat her with due style. [5]

To prevent an imbroglio I must bore you with a *fait divers*. On Wednesday, November 28, Miss Eugenie *Menter* (much more intelli*gent* than her famous older sister[6]) was to perform your op. 83 at a subscription concert in Munich. The day before, that hysterical lazybones of a conductor[7] sent me a telegram, asking me to send him the part and the score! I refused to do so, out of due respect for your work, or, let's say, for Simrock.

Please pass on friendly greetings to M. K.[8] It's not by chance that he lives on Beethoven Street, just as Sp.[9] should live on Herbeck's road.[10]

May The Nine watch protectively over—Euripides![11]

Till the end of this century, your loyal admirer

Hans v Bülow

No. 17

[8 January 1884]

Frankfurt/Main, 8 Jan. 84

Exalted Master,
Dearest Friend!

Two years ago today at the Sing-Academy[1] in Berlin I received from you a gift for which I congratulate myself every day, and especially today. The honor bestowed on me by your brotherly kiss has given the rest of my life worth and consecration.

That same year I lost my oldest, perhaps most fatherly friend,[2] whose memory I celebrate today. I met him in Stuttgart in 1846. My first public appearance as a boy at the piano occurred there on 8 January 1848. An unpublished piano fantasy on Kücken's Pretender (!) was the first propaganda I made for the man I miss today.[3]

In the midst of my grief (must I not just as egoistically as uselessly lament *almost* all of my active and passive experience from the past 37 years?) I rise and am revived by the thought of you, the thought of a *true* master that I acknowledged late, but (thank goodness!) not *too* late, the thought of a kind, lenient friend! Allow me to congratulate myself on that discovery; continue your benevolent friendship to me in this new phase of my life.

Looking up to you in firm, loyal admiration,

Your subservient

Hans v Bülow

No. 18

[12 January 1884]

> Nuremberg, where they don't
> hang everyone they catch. [1]
> Saturday, 12 Jan. 84

My great, dear friend!

"Another letter so soon?" Don't worry, this is simply a morning news, feuilleton-like personal note. Well, without knowing it, yesterday and the day before you made me very happy. Ludwig's Nos. 11 & 12 [2] enjoyed an unparalleled performance. The orchestra is possessed by such an enormous ambition and sense of honor that their overall verve and delicacy matches the best Vienna blood (without Galician-Semitic mélange). This state of continued, organized ecstasy is so becoming to your works that I desperately regret how slow cultural progress is: I cannot place a telephone call to the suburb of Wieden. You would have loved our performance! I begged the moment to "linger, please, it's so beautiful," [3] but all that remained is a hellish head cold that I hope the devil himself catches from me.

Tomorrow in Erlangen we will be playing your Academic Festival Overture despite Herzog's [4] nuzzling to get the third Lenore [*sic*] [5] eskimoed into the program. As you know, he has one of those difficult innately weathered authoritarian natures that knows no *divus* as long as he *vivus*.

I look forward very much to the 21st in Frankfurt/Main. [6] Couldn't you join us? That is, in case your auntie doesn't choose precisely that day to have a musical monster soirée in her home, as she did on January 7. [7]

Naturally, her intent was noble. She sought to protect Frankfurt's chaste lovers of music from my "attempted vivisections" of your forerunner. [8] *Tamen est laudanda voluntas.*

May I request something without upsetting you? Perhaps you could write yourself a little orchestra παρέργου, a little one-movement Fuchs serenade [9] or Grätener junior caprice? [10] You could dedicate it to our, well, your court orchestra. I say this because Pest-Weimar [11] has dedicated a Bülow March (!!!) to us. You can imagine the pleasure I take in fulfilling this forgotten ovation, notwithstanding the disdainful jokes that Dr. E. H. [12] will certainly make about the double father-in-law. You will understand my need for this sort of impersonal balsam. But then again, perhaps I will get over this new unmotivated march as I have done so many times before in my marching life and you may regard this expectoration as suppressible.

> With the deepest wishes for your well-being,
> In loyal admiration
> Your H v Bülow [13]

No. 19

[Postcard; Meiningen 28 May 1884]

Respected Master and Friend,

To spare you the suspense involved in opening an envelope, I'm using this plebian means of communication to put forth my (un)modest request that you reserve a seat for me in some hidden corner of the hall (anywhere will do) to hear the performance of your Third. I will be coming from Strasbourg to D[1] solely for that half hour.

Your most respectful, loving
V Bw

No. 20

[30 June 1884]

Frankfurt/Main, end of June
1884

Most esteemed friend!

How kind of Your Highness to think of me. I have difficulty repaying your "kiss on the hand" because I have no Domenico telling me pleasant things to write. I myself, namely, am somewhat off track and worn out. The piano teaching,[1] to which I am unaccustomed, did not bore me in the least, but since I pulled it off with my usual *troppo brio*, it caused considerable nervousness that I shall try to sleep off tomorrow in Meiningen.

I lack the self-confidence to say whether it was "worth the effort"!

Your publishers at least will certainly profit from it, although you may not prefer that for Small-Butt, Softie, and Mustard.[2]

There is, unfortunately, no lack of annoyances—here and elsewhere. But I did not allow Bernhard the Great[3] the pleasure of seeing me trip over the obstacles his clique put in my way.

Does that interest you?!!

Now, in November, for the *majorem gloriam et perenniam ducalem*, the court orchestra is to take an artistic journey during which—thanks to the ebullient guarantee-fury of Non-Simrock—the emperor's city will thrice enjoy your Third[4]: on Nov. 20, 25, and 29.[5] Will you be there then? If yes, tell me what you would least mind hearing me and my troupe perform for you.

Can one be more courteous? I will try to be so in the negative by not asking you, for instance, how you are or whether you are perhaps even composing a Fourth, for which Mrs. V. H.[6] at the Villa Carlotta[7] may have provided inspiration for lyrical secondary motifs. I'm happy for your "cousin" that you spent some time with him, he has probably been just as charming a host to you as he was not a charming employer on the Werra.

If I weren't faced with the pleasure of rehearsing F major,[8] I would be tempted to shout the name of Delibes's[9] last opera and make myself scarce to somewhere like Bayreuth minus the "e" [Beirut]. Hopefully there's no Wagner club there. As it is, all those Farzipalarians are starting to chirp at *me*.[10] May God Almighty protect Your Highness on all your ways and bridges (in the string quartet)—and if he does, I shall not refrain—despite my own personal rancor—from granting him also the title of Omni-benevolent.

Your loyal Knight of St. Johannes
Hans v Bw

No. 21

[Probably 9 October 1884[1]]
Most esteemed Friend!

Since for the pleasure of seeing your handwriting I am indebted after all to the nonpublisher of your F-major,[2] I will wish the *good man* back from Willenbacher,[3] to whom I had sent him in my thoughts.

Can you trust me? Hmm, hmm. You know what our Meiningen "specialty" is. If it were up to me, the program would be as follows:[4]

1. Beethoven Soirée.
2. Op. 90 F.
    Op. 68 Cm.
    Op. 73 D. (The order is intentional.)
3. Op. 81
    Op. 15
    Op. 56a
    Op. 83
    Op. 80

Since op. 15 and 83 require no conductor at all to run very smoothly and my fingers have now stretched sufficiently to reach the desired glove size, I thought I would be so brazen as to suggest either have *two* pianos play the solo part, or surprise the audience by reversing the announcement and dividing the performance among ourselves. Would you deign to conduct one (or two?) symphonies personally? No rehearsal necessary. We will do our fanatical best to let you have fun (or, rather, give you pleasure) and live up to your recommendation.

His Highness left the day before yesterday on a two-week trip to Meran.

For a while I have threatened to write, but modesty hindered me because I didn't wish to beg. But, what the devil, I'll gather my courage. Ignore and forgive if my respect for the dead implies disrespect for the even greater living. *Ecco di che si tratta*. Raff's widow has entrusted me with an oeuvre posthumously: four preludes for a large orchestra for *Macbeth*, *Othello*, *Romeo and Juliet*, and *The Tempest*. The score and arrangement for four hands at the piano are very careful clean copy.[5] Could you convince Simrock to print and worthily remunerate the work?

Do you mind if I play your concertos and conduct your symphonies in January on the Neva?[6] I won't don an *ushanka* just for the money. Or are you thinking of accepting an invitation there yourself? I've given up the Rhine and Holland for now. In March we plan to travel to East and West Prussia, but I need January and February to alleviate my own financial distress. I hope to have real fun next month in Munich as a counter-Levi.[7] This morning your Third went—forgive the strong word—heavenly. The individual practices: *hic haeret aqua.*[8]

Well, your reason for visiting the Styria is probably not to trouble yourself with letters from myself and Gutmann. Good-bye until six weeks from now.

In loyal admiration and devotion
Your H v Bülow

No. 22

[18 October 1884]

Meiningen, 18/X 84

Highly esteemed Friend,

I must thank you for your "golden," or should I say "steely" words in reply to what now appears to me to have been a fairly trivial importunity.[1] How thoroughly damn right you are! Although this moral portrait of yours does not surprise me (otherwise you would not, in my mind, be the great *man* that I admire), I am very pleased to own it penned in black and white and signed by you yourself.

But the feat of writing letters with one hand while packing your valise with the other[2] is a challenge to my imagination and skills and I shall endeavor to emulate you under the condition that your other local colleagues, Bachrich, Brüll, and Bruckner[3] have not already done so.

Regarding Gutmann,[4] I have decided to take the short straw. If I can, I shall relieve him of the responsibilities bound to his role as impresario. I hope you can at least passively support me on just *one* point: I find the third Lenore overture a little risky considering that we do not have an overabundance of "Quints"[5] in Vienna: I asked him to allow us to close the concert with your *Academic Overture* which we have drilled ourselves to play quite tolerably. Gutmann will ask Wolff[6] to ask you to glorify one of our two (Buda-)Pest concerts.[7] I would not have had the courage to do so.

My wife is touched and grateful that you thought of her recently and asks me to send you her most respectful greetings.

I just received Simrock's breve just in time: I already felt obligated to correct the score based on the viola variants.

On the 31st Steinbach[8] will perform your Third in Mainz. I believe I have already told you about this sensitive, yet strapping conductor. His orchestra is excellently disciplined, too. Recently they performed as guests in Wiesbaden and their local success was scary. If you ever are in that area, let me be so bold as to recommend that you hear them. Whether or not Levi[9] and Richter[10] approve, in my opinion Steinbach and Mottl[11] are the best orchestra conductors of the younger generation. I do not have to pack my suitcases yet, but you do probably have to unpack yours, thus I shall not add another word here.

May you find Vienna (Vindobona—*Wenden-Base?*[12]) as pleasant as always and allow me to most cheerfully look forward to our rendezvous in four weeks,

Your most loyal admirer,
Hans v Bw

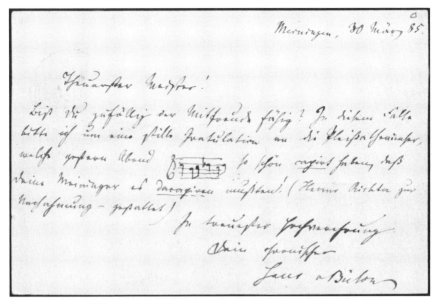

Postcard. *Staatsbibliothek zu Berlin—Preussischer Kulturbesitz; SBB Mus. Ep. Hans von Bülow 302*

No. 23

[Postcard, 30 March 1885]

Meiningen, 30 March 85

Dearest Master!

Can you share my joy? If yes, please silently congratulate the Pleissenland Athenians who last night *got*

so well[1] that your disciples in Meiningen had to *give* it to them again! (Hans Richter[2] may follow suit.)

In most loyal esteem,
chronically your,
Hans v Bülow

No. 24

[16 May 1885]

Berlin, 16 May
Hafenplatz 4

Esteemed, dearest Friend!

My wife has just handed me the jewel of an autograph with which you have so fabulously repaid my favor![1] How can I ever thank you? But you did miss one thing: You should have added to Beethoven's pencil a little Brahms's ink—*tres faciunt collegium.*

Thank you for so kindly accepting the little Hector,[2] I am proud to have filled a gap in your collection.

How odd that you would think that I, on the banks of the Werra, am resting on my laurels from the Newa and the Seine! No—I shall use the evening of my life to accomplish more than I did at dawn and noon. Now that I know which "kings are building," I shall dutifully "pull the cart" as best I can.[3] The enclosure will reveal how I'm spending the month of May: It's easy to keep busy when the weather's bad. In June, too, like unholy Dionysus I shall do penance for past and future sins—as a schoolmaster.[4] Incidentally, I myself benefit the greatest from it: From my pupils I learn how your works ought to be played.

I'd violate my own principles of friendship's respect, were I to ask out of curiosity what you're working on. And yet I can hardly conceal the effort it takes to keep my pen from wandering in that direction. It would be damn kind of you to at least once, *motu proprio*, give me some kind of clue.

Our faraway duke—in the fog on the Thames. Mannstädt is no longer conducting garden concerts in closed halls in Berlin.[5] I will probably let Richard Strauss voluntarily substitute for him during my vacation months of December (Petersburg) and January (Paris).[6] But none of this is final. In November I'll be parading *our* orchestra to Rhineland and Belgium.

Why don't you, for a change, visit Baden-Baden once again in the fall? There you'd find me and my wife, who greet you now with admiration,

Your
H v Bülow

No. 25

[16 September 1885]

Meiningen, 16 Sept. 85

Most highly esteemed Master and Friend!

I got your wonderful message [1] upon arriving home last evening. I cannot imagine anything more welcome than the honor of your visit. Come, practice, and do as you please! His Highness [the duke] will certainly demonstrate equal loyalty and take pride in your presence all the way up "to the *grand* duke."

The whole orchestra reassembles as usual on 1 October. Diligent practice is scheduled for mornings and afternoons. Our local subscription concerts on the Sundays of October 11, 18, and 25, and on 1 November will hardly disrupt things. On November 2 the orchestra leaves for a three-week tour to Frankfurt, Rhineland, and Holland; Baron von Wolff's fingers are black with ink from getting it all organized. He has not yet shown me the final plan and probably can't because it is all so complicated—*nulla dies sine concentu* [2]—and constantly undergoing change. But *during* your stay—*when* will that be?—everything will fall in place as it should.

Our entire time is at your disposal. I can also get two competent copiers for October. In short: *ai di Lei commandi!*

With respectful greetings from my wife,

In haste, your ever loyal servant,

Hans v Bülow

No. 26

[17 September 1885]

Meiningen, 17 Sept. 85

Distinguished Master and Friend,

not to bring bad news, but . . . yesterday morning I was poorly, i.e. insufficiently informed of matters ducal and municipal, so I must add something. I spoke to His Highness the Duke yesterday evening. With cordial ducal greetings he asks me to express his regret that your visit in October will benefit him *little*. Until a few days ago, Baroness von Heldburg has been *seriously* ill, suffering from meningitis, and while her health does seem to be improving, in the best case it could take not just weeks, but perhaps months. The duke "hopes to be able to attempt" moving the grand lady to Kissel (their hunting residence near Eisenach) in early October, and naturally her illustrious husband will accompany her. These autumn events naturally do not mean that the duke, whenever so inclined, will not visit Meiningen from time to time. Your presence will create an exceptional temptation to do so, but otherwise . . .

you will have to make do with us rather boring musicians, not to mention the unpleasant aspects of Thuringian cuisine, etc., etc.

Please excuse this revised "official" information, it alters nothing of my own personal reply yesterday, namely, that I consider your proposed visit—which will be *when?*—the most festive conceivable Epiphany.

Wishing you golden skies and blue sunshine for the remainder of your stay in the country,

Your loyal admirer,
H v Bülow

No. 27

[25? September 1885 [1]]

Esteemed Friend!

Excuse today's inconvenient telegram that I dispatched directly after getting your letter which I allowed myself to show to His Highness (it would have been profane to transcribe it). "Namely," I must decide on programs for our four inevitable local concerts on Oct. 11, 18, and 25, and Nov. 1. The duke wishes us to play mostly Beethoven because it draws the largest crowds. And we also have Strauss's [2] debut, etc., etc.

If I knew when you were coming, I could spare you one or another moment of boredom and put the orchestra entirely at your disposal; I could also invite Brodsky [3] to play your concert in your honor, etc., etc.

In short, I would be very obliged to you if you could set the date of your arrival.

Enclosed is the score planned for use on our November journey. Would you be so kind as to return it to me with performance indications and fingering?

Our flute player and secretary Abbass [4] will organize the matter of copying. Our best copyist (2nd bassoon) [5] is already available, three others will be available as of Oct. 1 so that we can finish it by Oct. 15.

Your new piece [6] could court public applause as early as the 25th, for instance, applause from your admirer Prince Alex of Hesse [7] (you know him from Wiesbaden); he'd like to attend our rehearsals in October. Baroness von Heldburg is improving at "a snail's pace" (as her celebrated spouse writes), but, as I said, it will take months. I reflect, reflect, and reflect again on replacement for Mozart's adagio for you and can find nothing. Should I send a telegram to Marseille? [8]

In loyal admiration,
Your servant
H v Bülow
Urgent—pardon!

No. 28

[7 October 1885]

Meiningen, 7 Oct. 85

Esteemed Friend!

Expect no misunderstandings or imbroglios *on my part*. My respect for your liberty is much too great.

But let me first answer your questions.

The copies will be completed by the *15th or 16th at the latest*. If necessary, I will relieve our best scribe, namely Truckenbrodt,[1] from his rehearsal duties and let the contrabass play the second bassoon in his place.

His Highness offers the little palace across from Hotel Saxon Court for your accommodation.

And finally, we expect you *as soon as you would like to come*.

In the second concert, on the 18th, Strauss will play Mozart's Concerto in C minor and direct his own Symphony in F minor. For the third concert, on the 25th, I have engaged Brodsky to play your violin concert. If you would like to direct that yourself, it would naturally be a great pleasure for him and all of us.[2] Otherwise, we shall rehearse and perform *whatever you wish*.

Early in the season the duke ordered me to perform mostly Beethoven in the hope that it would draw concertgoers from the banks of the Werra that otherwise stay home. Now the subscriptions have come in and I see myself bound to no other promise than the one I solemnly made to you—namely, not to bore you.

Need I tell you how happy and honored the duke, not to mention the rest of us (and not to mention the grinning royal treasurers), would be at his favorite musician's performing Symphony no. 4 (or an earlier one) with the Meiningen orchestra at the concerts in Rhineland and Holland?[3] As tempting as it has been for me, as the *curator*, to take up your offer for practical reasons [i.e., drafting programs for the tour], so far I have withstood it. I want to allow you the freedom to decide, once you have tried out your piece. It is not inconceivable that you may be dissatisfied with it or feel like changing it once it has been tried. Believe me, it would put me in an awkward position, because . . . His Highness . . . please be so kind as to read between the lines . . .

Apparently the duke's wife is again not well at their hunting residence in Kissel. The princess[4] thinks they will relocate to Altenstein, but is not certain; I myself can make neither heads nor tails of these strange arrangements. His Highness wishes to link two things that are not easily combined: marital care and a passion for nimrod. It annoys the duke to think that if he cannot do it himself, Saxe-Weimar will shoot the best game after first driving it from Meiningen to Eisenach grounds. But as soon as he knows you are here, he may stop brooding over it.

Forgive the careless confusion in this report; forgive even more my indiscrete inquiry of whether you would be inclined to conduct the Meiningen orchestra on November 3rd or 24th in Frankfurt? [5]

In any case, please be generally and particularly reassured
of the ever respectful devotion of your loyal servant,
H v Bülow

No. 29

[16 May 1886]

Frankfurt/Main 16/V 86

Most esteemed Master!

Contrary to habit, this time I haven't thanked you immediately for your kind lines, as common courtesy would have demanded. I thought it appropriate to first thoroughly research the whereabouts of the letter that Her Highness Princess Marie claims I received from you. [1] The result is absolutely nothing: a dead letter, as the English say. It is as lost as had it never arrived. As much as I am sorry about it, nothing can be done, and all that remains for me to do is to thank you cordially for your kind goodwill that prompted you to write although you (like Egmont in the scene with his secretary [2]) don't enjoy it.

But the explanation for the delay of this reply does not authorize me to overtax your correspondence-hostile eyes with more things. Besides, the wealth of material that you find so *un*interesting makes it difficult for me to decide what to write. I swear—by Willenbacher! [3]—that I did not know which of them you (duly) could not care less about. Allow me just to attach a prophylactic note: if I, *tant bien que mal*, continue to make propaganda for the beauty of your music, I do so by god not with any irreverent pretension of making you happy. I do it solely for *my own pleasure* (may others disapprove; that's part of it). *Anch' io sono*, while not *pittore*, indeed *egoista*. [4] Each as he can.

Allow me, by sending my most sincere wishes for your well-being,
to renew my unalterable esteem and admiration *in every way and respect*,
Hans v Bülow

No. 30

[17 March 1887]

Bonn on the Rhine, 17 March 87

Most esteemed Master!
Dearest Friend!

Last night following the *Tragic Overture* you inspired me to a good deed. [1] In priding myself on it, I am only saying that I am proud of you—since you are in need of it.

So, to get to the matter: At supper with the pots of the royal committee I readily agreed to their proposal to direct 10 concerts next season in Hamburg on the condition that I do *half* of them and C. R. take over the *other half.*[2] Any sympathetic observer can see the head concert attendant's embarrassing humiliation that it took little effort for me to clearly demonstrate. And the situation is particularly humiliating to the concert association itself: they are throwing away 29 years of musical culture in Bremen. Now, more of it is C. R.'s own fault than you may know or believe,[3] but nonetheless . . . with the help of the mayor and guild master and a few nice ladies I was able to make this deal. "Angel of peace Hanusch."[4]

Yesterday the Cologne quartet (Hollaender & Co.)[5] played your Sextet in G major here most charmingly. God, is the world of sound beautiful, when one can hear something of yours every day!

In most loyal admiration,
Your Bülow

My daughter[6] is starting to be converted. Thank god Countess Wolkenstein[7] is in Petersburg. My son-in-law[8] is a help to me.

One question: Who wrote the book on Mrs. Gottsched that you recently lent to me in Vienna?[9] I'd like Daniela to read it. *RSVP* to Hamburg, Waterloo Hotel, where I shall arrive on the 22nd and hammer away until the end of the month.

No. 31

[30 March 1887]

Hamburg, 30 March 1887

Esteemed Master! Dear Friend!

Please accept my twofold cordial thanks, first, for sending the nice gift to Bonn,[1] and second, for your kind reply.

The enclosure will prove that I am doing what is humanly possible.[2] It's terribly difficult to achieve what we want. A truly fanatic desire for injustice toward C. R. has swayed Bremen. I haven't given up trying to bring these people to reason. But the large paying majority currently prefers to "practice" ostracism.

Prof. Claus Groth[3] arrived here yesterday. He was seriously ill for a long time, you can still tell. Unfortunately, he was unable to attend the recent Spengel[4] concert. His physician says he had "malaria," a kind of Maremma[5] fever. He sends you enthusiastic greetings.

In a rush,
in great adoration, your loyally subservient admirer,
Bülow

No. 32

[23 May 1887]

Frankfurt/Main, 23 May 87
Hotel Swan

Highly esteemed Master,
Dear Friend!

The sight of your pen marks turns the coldest day of May into the merriest of January. I send my swift thanks! For almost two weeks I have been working exclusively on op. 99 ff.,[1] rehearsing both here and in Wiesbaden with various inadequate cellists, but more tolerable violas. The last time was yesterday in Rüdesheim, where I, to my own great satisfaction, went through both of your violin sonatas with your old loyal and kind admirer Mr. Von Beckerath[2] (under the personal surveillance of St. Cecelia of Nerotal[3]). An amateur is sometimes quite refreshing! An amateur really studies the *piece*, not just the *role* he is to play, as does the professional orchestra craftsman, who usually (instinctively?) plays the best when sight-reading and then gets uneasy and worse with each additional rehearsal.

Now to my personal impression: As is so often the case with your "things," it takes me the longest to grasp the ones that are most comprehensible. Now, for instance, the violin sonata keeps going so pleasantly through my mind, while at first I found the trio and even the cello sonata better. Believe me, these three new works are not "posthumous," and even if you presently don't feel like exclaiming "παντα λιαν"[4] in emulation of Jehovah's certified review of creation, the German public, educated by you, would not be unwise to snatch up these new pieces faster than ever like "soft, warm Lent pretzels."

Your traveling companion in Italy—I mean the worldling,[5] not the little prophet[6]—will, with this new help from you, soon be able to purchase another showpiece for his picture gallery—or my name's "Hanusch."[7]

My traveling companion in Italy, of whom you strangely heard, was—you're absolutely right—a piano student I by chance discovered before breakfast in Venice "25 years ago" in the *trattoria orientale* (behind Piazza San Marco; with exquisite ultramontane cuisine). Frits Hartvigson,[8] a Danish Jew, a very nice, but aesthetically uneducated chap who lived in London and was renowned for his self-sacrificing work at the Institute for the Blind at Upper Norwood, as you've probably heard. (He once also taught Hesse's blind nobleman.[9]) I suggested one day that he accompany us to Bologna, do sightseeing at torre Asinelli and campo santo (magnificent) and see Mrs. Mutzenbecher as Raphael's original.[10] It went quite well, in the evening we even had the rare pleasure of seeing trained "geese" (really!) perform at the circus. Besides that, B. has the nicest, cleanest, and cheapest Hotel Albergo del Pellegrino (not to be confused with dei tre Pellegrini), where Lord Byron [11] wrote poetry in August and September 1819.

Isn't the commemorative plaque beautiful for once?

Qui

in Agosto e Settembre MDCCCXIX albergò e per la libertà Giorgio Gordon
Lord Byron che alla Grecia la vita
all' Italia diè il cuore e l'ingegno
del quale
niuno surse tra i moderni più potente d'accompagnare alla poesia l'azione, niuno più
inclito e pietoso a cantare le glorie e le sventure
del nostro popolo.

———

A ricordo con gratitudine d'italiano
Francesco Ravaldoni pose 1887.★

★According to the most recent edition of Baedeker.

Isn't that well said, despite all pathetic corpulence? Well, it wasn't written by the best author, but by the last best Italian poet Jose Carducci, [12] professor in Bologna.

"Let me heartily recommend the restaurant to you"—the owner insisted that I do.

By the way, Carl Reinecke is going to the Silesian music festival to patch up his disagreement with Schaeffer. [13] Theodor K. [14] has probably already informed you. But unfortunately our friends from Wiesbaden and Rüdesheim will be rhapsodizing their way to the Dusseldorf event, presumably they don't yet know about your Academic Overture. This time I, however, am going to Cologne, but will naturally be staying (with my daughter [15]) in Bonn; I'll listen to some things by telephone only, others, like Berlioz's *Romeo & Juliet* I'll hear in greater physical proximity. *Presently I would like so much to know whether the rumor is true that you plan to personally perform your new chamber music works at one of the chamber music soirees.* [16] Please be so kind as to simply scribble "no" or "yes" on any old postcard and send it to me. I would be so very, very grateful if you did.

With 101 [17] greetings and best wishes, your cordially loyal,
subservient admirer,
H v Bülow

No. 33

[27 May 1887]

Frankfurt/Main 27 V 87

Highly esteemed Master and Friend!

You have spoken from the depths of my heart and so refreshingly ranted and railed Faust's rape in Cologne[1] that I must thank you immediately. Just imagine, many in the trade swallow the rubbish because of its sterling aura! The worst is that the K.M.G.V.[2] is totally degenerating because their conductor is so preoccupied with selling himself as an author that he neglects his practical professional duties.

Thank you for letting me know that you will play your trio yourself, oh, I guess I should send my thanks to Barbarossa at Cologne's Kaiserring.[3]

I mean "Bismarck's" Billi,[4] currently district administrator in Hanau (not the member of the board of museums, but from the nest of the same name), who should more accurately be called "bun"-mark.[5] In comparison, twenty-five year-old concert and opera director Damrosch[6] from New York is a very charming, most intelligent, *modest*, and studious chap, who, if you should meet him, would probably not be a *nuisance*, but a *pleasure* to you.

Please be so kind as to read the enclosed newspaper clipping from Bremen so that no one can say I boasted or that I neglected the plans I mentioned in March.[7] Well then, good-bye until the Cologne choir concert in four weeks. By the way, to avoid the crock devotees,[8] I am staying at Hotel Royal in Bonn (Mrs. C. M.[9] from Wiesbaden will be there, too). Perhaps you could do the same.

Loyally, your most admiring, subservient
Bülow

No. 34

[13 January 1888]

Hamburg 13 I 88

Highly esteemed Master!

Just two lines to confirm having received the score for your double concerto yesterday. The so-called right hand is still half invalid, but I will have it back in shape by February 6th so that Joachim and Hausmann[1] can rehearse conducting the accompaniment, since you choose not to do Mr. Wolff the honor or give him the pleasure of directing your work at his concert yourself.

Though I'm neither a chimney sweep nor a night watchman, I take this occasion for the triviality of wishing you a consoling leap year 1888, as your
Reverent, subservient admirer
H v Bülow[2]

No. 35

[15 November 1888]

Hamburg 15 Nov. 88

Most highly esteemed Master!

    I never dreamt I'd be indebted to wonderful Mrs. d'Albert[1] for the rare honor of a message from you. I envy her! Your kind lines[2] reached me *a tempissimo*[3] last night at the concert hall and gave me the welcome and direly needed encouragement to risk (under rather complicated "local circumstances" (Ibsen)[4]), and thank heavens, to succeed at performing your *Haydn Variations* which inspired the audience *and* the orchestra to mentally and physically applaud the absent *author* (sic! as the journalist says).

    "When the kings, etc. . . . ,"[5] it makes your most loyal wagon driver exceedingly happy that by taking up residence at Alsterglacis no. 10 he not only has a beautiful view, but also the prospect of seeing you sometime this winter when you visit your hometown to inspect the changes induced by the new customs arrangements. Could you not, at your convenience, let us know beforehand approximately when that will be?

    Here, on January 10 in the fourth [subscription] concert, masters Joachim and Hausmann[6] will perform your double concerto. The former could not enthusiastically enough assure us how embarrassing it is for him to have to disappoint his Avé[7] of many, many years by not performing under Prof. Von Bernuth's[8] "direction"; for the sake of Hermann Wolff, to whom he had firmly given his promise, I concealed my trepidation and resignation and decided to perhaps settle for HH Brodsky[9] and Klengel,[10] who I believe achieves stronger half-note triplets on the C string.[11]

    On February 7 in the fifth [subscription] concert I shall direct your Academic Overture,[12] on February 22 in the sixth [subscription concert] I shall perform your opus 15 (perhaps letting your friend Spengel take the baton);[13] in an extra concert on March 11 we shall reminisce with your third symphony.[14] Depending on when you choose to come, I could let your presence be "celebrated" (forgive me!) by performing whichever of your works you are the least "disinterested" to hear. I shall wait for your orders. You might have the pleasure of seeing Ignatz Brüll's "Stone Heart"[15]—silver brooch—here at the theater. One cannot know fate's favor or disfavor in advance.

    À la cour il faut être court, Liszt once said to Karl Alexander; so I shall content myself with cordially thanking you again for sending vital signs and not pester you with greetings from my venerable co-wagon drivers from the New Free and the Press,[16] remaining—until Gotha—with great respect

Your loyal
Hans v Bülow

No. 36

[31 January 1889]

Hamburg, ultimo Jan. 89

Sire!

I scribble today, not to send condolences regarding the country's k. k. grief,[1] but to share my joy at the nice performance of your opus 102 two days ago in Bremen, though it naturally means naught to you. What the devil: I continue to live ever in your "entire works" (for instance, tomorrow we shall rehearse opus 11 in Berlin, today we are doing opus 90 here) and must give their creator a vital thankful sign once again.

Are you coming? When?

But now getting back to Bremen: Both chaps[2]—the *ignostissimi*—gave their stirringly bustling best. Skill grows to meet the task. In the end they played your work for me less professorially and academically, as it were, less snobbish and more youthfully audacious than the Mono-Metropolitans have done up to now. They repeated the middle part—and that has never been done here in your town of birth.

May God sustain you for me and Simrock for you. If one doesn't see the world of music in one's publisher, well . . . and so on.

After trying for so long to win J. J.'s[3] favor, I followed Richter's[4] example and by decently performing his Kleistian overture[5] finally got a word of recognition from him. Triumph song.

I Mei rispetti your dynastic opponents H. and K.[6] The first of the two brought me to tears with his sacrificing notes on opus 102.[7] Bacchus dances. Two steps forward, one back. He probably thought he had gotten overly enthusiastic in reviewing your new *Lieder*[8] and now had to save his Rhadamanthine reputation of being objective and impartial. Well, enough.

With heartfelt wishes for your well-being,
Your loyal, chief admirer and obedient contemporary
Bülow

My wife, who sings you[r songs] rather well, sends devoted greetings.

No. 37

[24 May 1889 [1]]

Wiesbaden, St. John's Day 89

High Master,
dearest Friend!

You will surely see why I waited for your rise in status to sincerely thank you for the lift in status that you have awarded me by dedicating your beautiful sonata in D minor to my person. [2] It took longer than expected for the first to come into effect; at fault were once again none other than these local, or should I say, unfortunate circumstances . . . (Rumors of objections were canard, fable, and nonsense!). At least that is what fine, old mayor Peterson [3] solemnly swore to me the day I returned from New York, May 14th. Said doge, incidentally, acted wonderfully in this matter that he himself engineered *proprio motu* and for which he deserves the warmest thanks from all your admirers and friends. I shall do my part by directing a so-called music festival in the exhibition hall—something I would otherwise dread. Well, we'll do things differently than is custom on the Lower Rhine, meaning: no Messiah and no Ninth. On each of the three days we'll perform a work of yours and one by Mendelssohn, you're kin by the cradle, and a little bit of C. Ph. Em. Bach to commemorate his dying on 14 September 88 in Hamburg. The first half of September, namely, is when this all will probably take place. May we be so disrespectful as to invite you? I'm *afraid*, namely, that the event will be neither beautiful nor correct.

But getting back to that honorable mayor of yours [now that you are a citizen of Hamburg]: Petersen is turning 80 on 6 July of this year. In his opening speech (it was a *capolavoro* [masterpiece]) at the exhibition he denied the words sent by our Imperial Prince Chancellor to Carl Schurz: alas, dear friend, the *first* seventy years of one's life are by far the best. (That is authentic.) Perhaps you could congratulate him by telegram on that day. I myself would have sent you one on 7 May, but I was afloat on the "Fulda," equidistant from both continents. I brought you something for your library, hoping you don't already own them, namely two rare (?) items by Boieldieu: scores for *Voitures verses* and *Chaperon rouge*, [4] which I have had Böhme [5] send to Vienna. But enough details. Madame Cécile hourly laments the death of your former landlady [6] here and hopes to see you "without an appendix" (I believe that malice was mine) when your fifth symphony is performed in Berlin.

Farewell, dear, dear Master, and as long as we don't provoke it,
don't forget your loyal and your most faithful
Hans v Bülow
(who no longer envies Billroth [7]) [8]

No. 38

[4 June 1889]

Wiesbaden, 4 June 89
Black Bear

High Master,
dearest Friend!

to spare you worry, I sent a telegram yesterday confirming the receipt of your—once again—strikingly grandiose new piece.[1] I got notice [of the roll] from the post office on Saturday evening, but the customs office is closed on Sunday, etc. I'll send the sheets (by registered mail, of course) to Böhme[2] today so that he can hand them over directly to your friend Spengel. It all depends on when the Cecilia Association[3] takes vacation, I hope not before July. It would be wonderful if your rehabilitated hometown were to have the pleasure of the premier performance!

I will have to write your friendly greetings to my wife; she is with her ill mother in Cracow. But Mrs. Cécile[4] ardently returns your thoughts. This afternoon we plan to visit felicitous Madame Von Beckerath[5] in Rüdesheim, whom I shall greet from you without you asking me to.

Since I have absolutely *nothing* more to write that would interest you (I assume you are indifferent to my masseur), I am simply sending a hanseatic document[6] that pertains to you, but for which I refuse to take responsibility, as they say.

Your most loyal admirer,
Bülow

No. 39

[2 July 1889]

Hamburg, 2 VII 89

High Master and Friend!

Forgive my barging into your *villeggiatura** rather unannounced; I do so solely in my capacity as your backup calendar.

On the *6th* of July (= *this month*) your honorable mayor will be celebrating his 80th birthday for the first and last time. If you, who have often written him letters, are inclined to crown those by telegraphing him congratulations, this would be the opportunity.

Your friend of many years, Mr. Spengel is said to be rehearsing your chorus parts with the handsomest ambition. Since I felt it advisable and fair to assign to him the public directing of your festival piece, I would neither visit the rehearsals nor offer my own two cents and blessings,[1] even if the cold that I caught on my trip home didn't prevent me from doing so.

If the request's not indiscreet, may I allow myself to "intuit" whether you meant your promise (?) to honor the so-called music festival on 9, 11, and 13 September with your presence seriously, i.e., whether you will keep it.[2]

I've adjusted the program to the "local circumstances," as Ibsen put it so well.[3] Hm! Nothing but German names, nothing particularly difficult, wintry, one shorter or longer piece of yours and your "compatriot" Mendelssohn every day and a *sinfonietta* by Hamburg's Bach († 14 Sept. 1788), and to top it off, two old waltzes by young Strauss: *Volkssänger* [op. 119] and *Wings of Phoenix* [op. 125], and so on.

Dealing with music delegate Mr. Lavi is, among other things, very instructive. They want to make money, not deficits. It may characterize this Jew to say that he and the citizenry disagreed with the views of the senate and doge. Mr. Spengel and Mr. Krug[4] threaten to give you a homage speech with decorations by Hulbe.[5] I asked them to omit my name. All this club stuff and Philistine humbug disgusts me more every day and since I also devotedly declined the laggardly offer pushed on me to become an honorary member of Bonn's Beethoven House Association (Verdi, Hochberg, why not Czibuka and Nessler,[6] too?), you probably won't take my being consistent personally.

I have to tell you that in Hamburg we shall not, as is the custom, thresh the Ninth or other imperial nonsense. "Casuar"[7] has done it sufficiently in Cologne and Kiel with similar deficits. Nor shall we fiddle for more than two hours. Thus I shall not refuse, if in September you should decide to personally examine the temperature along the *Speckgang*,[8] which would very much please

Your ever most loyal admirer

Bülow

No. 40

[7 December 1889]

Berlin, 7 Dec. 89

Noble, dear Master and Friend!

Blessed be the folds on the face of the potted trumpeter,[1] who once again delivered lines written by your hand. Where, again, does the Pentateuch say "they saw God, and did eat and drink"?[2] Any sign that you have thought of me always refreshes my *appetite for life*, just when it was dwindling.

Ultimately, all Speidel's[3] loathsome things that you sent gave me the welcome opportunity to pay back kind with kind, or not-kind if you will. *At first*, out of weakness, I wasn't angry about them (for a long while I've turned anger only against myself), I just brooded. Really! You see, even if Mrs. and Mr. Von Herzogenberg[4] (*relictis ceteris*) admire you more intelligently, they cannot show deeper love for you than I. You illuminated my mind: The world of music owes to you everything praiseworthy that the last and best years of my life can offer! I don't know in what mood these lines will reach you, but don't smile more sunnily or grimly at this declaration of love than the doge of Hamburg did at your thank-you telegram for the honorary citizenship. The old man is wonderful: I meet him more often now and he does go to concerts that include your things.

Tomorrow night I shall travel to Hamburg to rehearse and finalize the program for the 12th. [5] The Double Concerto should, for the first time, really *ignite enthusiasm*; lately, for instance, we thoroughly "chiseled" its heavenly spherical closing passage. You know, don't scold me for being presumptuous, but to make the latent fire in your works become patent (obvious) [6] has become the favorite task, the hobby, of your most loyal

Little Baton
Bülow

P.S. I have a request, whose originality may let you forget its impertinence. I am approaching an ominous date, the completion of my 12th lustrum. I shudder at the thought of the practical jokes I'll endure: I'm not an old man (celebrate or groan—*au choix*). Comfort me by a telegram saying you are and will remain my friend! Please?

[Written on the back in blue pencil:] Sorry! I had no other stationery. [7]

No. 41

[16 December 1889 [1]]

My esteemed, dear Master!

Trembling and hesitating, the pen takes control of me: for the first time in my "*life as a night watchman*" (Aeschylus—Achilleis) [2] I am committing a *crimen laesae* on you by introducing a musician to you who can perhaps recommend himself, as he so kindly asked me to do in the enclosure. [3]

If you don't like him at all, you can pass him on to one of your alphabet colleagues in Vienna, e.g., *uckner* or *üll*. [4] Don't be too angry, I won't do it again, and won't say Schindler [5] *redivivus*.

Your *tuissimo* Bülow
Berlin, on Ludwig I's 119th birthday.

Enttäuschung.

Auf die Enthüllungen des Herrn Wilhelm Tappert in seinem Feuilleton »Acht Tage in Hamburg« bezüglich der Vorgeschichte meiner Ausweisung aus dem Berliner Opernhause entgegne ich Folgendes:

Zehntausend Mark baar zahle ich sofort an die Herren „Robert und Bertram" (s. Deutscher Bühnenalmanach, Altenburger Hoftheater) als milden Beitrag zur Minderung des Deficits beim nächsten schlesischen Musik.... feste, sobald das jenes Vorkommniss rechtfertigen sollende „amtliche Aktenstück" produzirt wird. Zugestanden, lieber Almariva: keine Dichtung ohne Wahrheit. Richtig ist, das ich auf die Rückseite des mir nach Meiningen 10. April 1884 zugestellten „Hofpianistenprädikatsentziehungsdecrets" die von Herrn Tappert citirte Antwort zu meinem Privatplaisir skizzirt habe — das Dokument ist mir durch einen Autographenliebhaber — kurz darauf — abhanden gekommen. Jedoch ist diese Skizze „Kladde" (Brouillon) geblieben; sie hat nimmer eine Reinschrift erfahren, ist also auch nimmer an ihre Adresse abgesendet worden. Ergo hat sie nimmer als „Epistel" von der hochseligen k. pr. Hausministerexcellenz empfangen und in hochderen Nachlass aufgefunden werden. können.

HAMBURG, ult. November 1889.

Dr. Hans von Bülow.

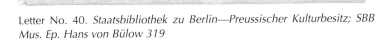

Letter No. 40. *Staatsbibliothek zu Berlin—Preussischer Kulturbesitz; SBB Mus. Ep. Hans von Bülow 319*

No. 42

[23 December 1889]

Hamburg 23 XII 89

Dearest Master!

I Moses, Ch. 24, v. 11.[1]

108 thanks for 73.[2] Yes, the beautiful book is part of it: You realize, I hope, that I fought back tears the first time I heard the B-major adagio. That was the epoch-making Damascus moment that turned me from an *S* (half eradicated anyway) to a *P*.

In a few days you will have to give me a bill of indemnity: I have misused your name in a bit of writing (?).[3]

"Now, don't exaggerate, in the end it will not have been *that* bad" commerce councilor Cohn said after hearing that commission counselor Meier had just died of *galloping* consumption. Wasn't it you who told me that story?

But the end justifies the means: Arm in arm with you I *could* simply rein the next decade into its becoming bounds, but instead you will become popular (sic!) in the Empire of Japan with its 40 million inhabitants, not counting idiots like Speidel, who misread prefixes and, as it happened in Leipzig, reprimand Goldmark for composing an overture to the lost idyll of Aeschylus!!![4]

My God, how great is Thy zoo! Enclosed are a few rather amusing bits of immortal nonsense (they don't mention your name) to encourage you to once again sometime send me a few things by the newspaper lice![5]

May you preserve all your wits, you wonderful commander
of the soul of your most loyal
Hans.

No. 43

[29 December 1889]

Hamburg, 29 Dec. 89

High Master, Dear Friend!

Kings have difficulty imagining the life of the wagon driver.[1] At the elevation where you stand, things are clear; down in the musty valley it's more complicated, "smellier."

As the year draws to a close it's my habit to clean up a bit, sort the trash, and so on. And I've discovered something that needs attending, regarding you, too. *Ecco*:

You have heard, anyway, that to achieve your upgrade to honorary citizen we had to overcome some resistance from dull circles. We have never discussed this point. I refrained particularly for the very good reason that (I was in Wiesbaden at the time of the debates) the issue seemed somewhat strangely obscure and I wanted to avoid *useless* questioning out of concern that it might at some point become *damaging*.

Finally, thanks to a good friend, I have discovered the gist of the matter: it's trifling, but poisonous.

Thus I am showing it to you. Feel free to show it to Ed. H. and K.,[2] too, and make a copy if you want, *but* I must ask you to return the file to me because I am obliged to do the same. In the world of music, the Polonius in question is actually known only as the publisher of "Queen of Saba" by C. G. Because he did not get "Merlin," he satisfies his yearning for celebrity by editing the "Hamburg Signals" (biweekly "two cents" in large format), which, in association with Tappert, throw dirt at you and your followers *almost* monthly.[3] I have punished T severely, as you know, with a lawsuit (he had to pay 600 marks) for the foul things that he wrote about you at every opportunity in Berlin's *Kleines Journal* [Little Journal].[4] Now *you're* rid of him—his complete rage is aimed at my "Monade."

Well . . . *già troppo—non raggionam' più di loro*, as Dante says in Alighieri.[5]

I assume you did receive Böhme's paper.[6] You will amnesty me? Baronial lords generally do that on New Year's Day.

May you not draw a blank [in the New Year's lottery] for yourself and thus for us in 1890!

Your, even more in the new decade than in the old, most loyal
Bülow

No. 44

[17 January 1890]

*Kant*opolis, Marzipanopolis
17 January 1890

My dear Master and honorable Friend!

I swept a bit here yesterday at the bleak spruce tree line (not at all leathern)[1] and had some luck, thanks to the valiant seventy-threes (read 73s). Swept away are the annoying pertinacious memories of St. Anthony from P. (not Padua), I mean the Attila of the worldly symphony and sacred opera.[2] Joined later by the solo parts and the whole choir (Bargiel, Herzogenberg, Rudorff, Thieriot, etc.[3]), I think it will turn out quite chic.

By the way, the community here has grown considerably, compared to years ago. Prof. Mikulicz, Billroth's fine pupil and friend, and Prof. Hermann, Hirschfeld (archeologist, discoverer of Hermes), the editor of the (national-liberal) Königsberg General Newspaper, Wyneken, and others, for example the brilliant Brahms-singer Mrs. Simon (*quondam* Mrs. Consul Ravené from Berlin)—well, that's enough.[4]

From Berlin I was only able to thank you by wire for your princely package on the 8th because I hadn't seen it until I returned home to Hamburg on Sunday. [5] My wife was just as pleased with it as was

> Your profoundly loyal loving
> Bülow

Sorry that I have no better stationery in my folder, [6] like national mourning stationery. Words, words—perhaps the song "without words" (you surely aren't familiar with it) would be more welcome.

No. 45

[24 January 1890]

Hamburg, 24 I 90

Dearest Master,

I don't own the Chrysander articles. [1] Spengel had lent them to me and I asked him right away to send them to you immediately.

Many thanks for the forceful and yet always so elegant renouncement [by] E. H. [2] I'll have several copies of it circulated to help outvote the subject [so] damaging to the public. Things like this make life sour: as your honest agent, I have no need of dishonest agents. "Goldman" versus "Tin Boy" has already become a dictum. The flea deserves it.

Did you get my letter from Königsberg? Not to be so insolent as to expect a reply. The day we left, I still had time to rehearse op. 102. Brode [3] and the cellist Heberlin [4] played quite decently. In the fall I shall return to stage the première. [5]

Your East Prussian Brahmins plan something very honorable. They intend to write a letter of thanks to mayor Petersen for awarding you the status of honorary citizen. That will please the elderly gentleman.

Now, forgive me for an inevitable request. Please return the circular by Mr. Hugo Pohle. [6] The member of the citizenry, who lent it to me, has asked to have it back. Or did you not receive my letter that contained it?

I've got a bad case of the flu that I seriously must cure because I have no time to be ill. On Monday I must return to Berlin, and so on. What nice people your Budapesters are! Aren't the Viennese plant lice [feuilleton writers] a little ashamed?

Give my most respectful regards to Prof. Hanslick when you see him.

> As always, with the most loyal, subservient admiration,
> Your deeply grateful
> Bülow
> /:Be prepared for a pleasant surprise!:/

In Königsberg Mrs. Gustav Simon (née von Kusserow, divorced Ravenè (Berlin)), an amateur, sang a number of your *Lieder*—old and new—positively ravishingly. In comparison, Hermine[7] is vermin.

You *must* go there sometime. It will refresh you. Dömpke[8] is a fine apostle!

My wife is *enormously* pleased by your picture.

Spengel seriously wants to leave here and is campaigning, despite advice, in all parts of Dusseldorf. He seems to fear that Jul. Stockhausen[9] will follow his plan to settle here again.

No. 46

[30 January 1890]

Berlin 30 I 90

Esteemed dear Master and Friend!

Your letters and cards were forwarded to me here [in Berlin], where I've been fooling around since Monday. I had a "white" night that I used to reconsider your .[1]

For this last decade I am determined to play the Fabian (cunctator) even less than in previous years: For most bipeds *cunctando destituit rem* is probably more true than *cunctando restituit rem*. Thus my chest note to you:

Yes.

(I need not express my thanks that you have been so kind as to not suggest that I support any "con"-servatory.)[2]

Now, as to the means to the end: Ask your apt Mr. Von Edi[3]—the stylist *par éminence*—to get things going and explain who and what Goldmann[4] is. Let him head it and I'll help.

Period.

I had a pleasant surprise the day before yesterday. J. J.[5] played a new quartet by H. v. H.,[6] I liked the score in F minor very much, much better than anything I've heard by him so far. I think you'd applaud it, too. They played it charmingly, but did a less charming job with op. 127 in E-flat major;[7] literally playing to the note could not compensate for the lack of intellectual warmth. The gentlemen seemed to have played it better when they were with you.

So, now you will have had enough. I feel a need to write to you and if I keep it *short*, you will forgive me more *often*. I *never* expect you to answer, although naturally I *always* am happy when you do, your

Most loyal baton,

H v Bw

/:5 Feb. in Hamburg, Serenade in D major!:/[8]

No. 47

[6 February 1890]

Hamburg, 6 II 90

My dearest Master!

Heavens! Your Serenade in D certainly is work! In the same amount of time I can prepare two of your symphonies, or at least get the details much better. Anyway, it was beautiful and the mayor—who arrived just as the adagio was ending—was more moved than ever before by anything your [servant, i.e. Bülow] has performed.★

[At the bottom of the page:] "★His true passion is for Norma and Figaro.¹"

Well, I hope these new impressions will be followed by naming a street after you.

Today I myself am exhausted. Unfortunately, I had to call off a concert in Munster and am writing in a state of fever, and ask you, please, in light of these aggravating circumstances (by the way, are there any other than aggravating circumstances?) to have the clemency of a friend with my penmanship. But now, getting to the Chrysander-ology!

The matter itself is settled. How to execute it, is the question. We should decide soon upon the mode.

1. *As far as I am concerned*, I would make the sum from Hamburg available to you, the prime person involved, and *you* would give it to *him*. *Noblesse* (honorary citizenship) *oblige*.
2. We could do it together, four-handedly. The moral image would be better than the material photograph from Leipziger Street!² You could write me two lines about Chrysander and I would reply with enthusiastic approval of your proposal and then send the minister and the chamber together to Bergedorf³ with those two letters and the ten thousand.
3. *Tertium non datur.*

In other words, Mr. v. Edi should organize it, and you and I are the second and third player—three makes a team.

It's your decision! I'll wait for the cue from you,

Your loyal vassal,
Bülow

If I'm free of fever tomorrow (which may happen), I shall travel to *Berlin* (Hotel Askan.) to direct the first philharmonic concert. On *Tuesday* morning I'll be on my way to Cöthen, on *Wednesday* to Greiz. From *Thursday* the 13th until *Saturday evening*, the 15th, I'll be in Weimar (Hotel Erbprinz). On *Sunday* I'll return here for concert rehearsals, etc. I'm writing this schedule to you now so that you can expedite your reply such that I get it without delay because *this matter must be taken care of before I leave* for America on 12 March. *Di doman' non v'ha certezza*, as Lorenzo de' Medici[4] sings. Perhaps you should compose something for that sometime when you have a bit of leisure. Ed. H.[5] can surely give you the text of the whole (short) Florentine song.

No. 48

[22 October 1890]

Hamburg, 22 Oct. 90

Esteemed, beloved Master and kind Friend!

That recent, incorrect quotation,[1] has probably already given you an idea of the sad shape my brain is in after months of ordeal. . . . I cannot pick up the pen without lapsing into an intolerable jeremiad . . . so I put it down again quickly. I have done it several times already when I, very touched, wanted to kiss your hand in thanks for your greetings. *Moriens te salutat*—yes, no pathos intended, but that is what I tried to write.

Just Monday evening[2] I was galvanized by quite a decent performance of your first symphony and felt—optimistically—redeemed. Yesterday and today have made it very clear to me that redemption can only mean release. I am totally exhausted, naturally it is my own fault. But our late emperor set a worthy example by only accepting *la* for *labor*, not for *lamenting*.

I dare to claim you would have enjoyed seeing the almost transfigured faces of the orchestra musicians while playing your works! And the old, 81-year-old doge, who considers you the second Bellini!—(formerly his favorite composer[3]), listened with fervid excitement, particularly during the finale, when our new flutist (Tieftrunk, a defector from Bernuth's camp[4]) intoned the redeeming motif[5] with enthusiastic coloration that I have never heard before: An inner sunrise on an old face can be very beautiful! That's how it was. Following the concert, incidentally, your honorary mayor invited us to his summer residence. Good heavens, that's Moltke-style, isn't it?

Well, out of desperation I have let the mole rummaging in my skull ramble on with words as Bruckner does with notes. To the flames! In all my still bright moments, until the last fire bursts or goes out, I reverently remain loyal to your genius and person,

Bülow

No. 49

[8 January 1891]

Berlin 8 I 91

Great Master and esteemed Friend!

Don't let the black border shock you, unfortunately I can't announce that one of your smallest followers has passed away.

No, I have a message that you will hopefully find more welcome. Recalling your great kindness from 8 January last year it occurs to me that I am equally greatly indebted to you. Well then, since I still can, I shall repay you today. Simultaneous to these lines I am also sending a letter to Bergedorf offering, in your name and mine (*suum cuique* and *viribus unitis*[1]), to Dr. Chrysander the amount of 1,000 crowns, collected by local friends of the arts and given to me to use for an artistic purpose that I deem worthy, as a contribution to the continuation of his mission in cultural history. Forgive that I used your name (I said that I *sought your advice*); it seemed necessary to ward off refusal.

I was very happy to hear from our splendid fellow D'Albert[2] better news of your state of health[3] than I had recently gotten from someone else. May the gods long keep you whole for the welfare of the world of music and perhaps for their own pleasure! That is the only prayer with which I, otherwise antagonistic, pester the divine.

Your most loyal
H v Bw

A little friendship has developed between myself and your old friend Th. K.,[4] whose real enthusiasm for you is equally fresh and refreshing. When my ailments allow it, the two of us go for bouillon at the Alster Pavilion in the mornings. For his sake (I'm so tired of the "masses" that I have respect solely for individuals of some significance) I have conducted diverse works by R. Sch.[5] with as much enthusiasm as if you had composed them yourself.

By the way, I hardly need ask you not to think that the doge's daughter's impatience (presently infatuated by mediocre violinist Z) is my fault.[6] Through the kindness of J. J. I was recently able to hear your wonderful Quintet in G major in Berlin[7] during the second-to-last rehearsal.

No. 50

[11 January 1891]

Berlin 11 I 91

Exalted Friend,

I fear we—pardon!—I fear *I* have made a fool of myself! You did get my note from the 8th and know what I'm talking about? Sixty hours later, and still no reaction from Bergedorf. Should Chrysander turn down my— unbefitting—imposition and be so indignant as to find it even unworthy of expressing a rejection?[1] Well, I am very disturbed and anxious about it. Of course, unrelenting physical pain tends to blow psychological discomfort all out of proportion. My donation letter to Chrysander may have been too casual, but in terms of "devotion" it left nothing to be desired.

Thus if your ink well flows generously, please do me the favor of exerting a little friendly pressure on Chrysander. Either you yourself, or via E. H., whose recent diatribe on Ibsen I liked better than the certainly unmerited pampering of Abraham's pet.[2] I find that Nordic—as far as I'm concerned— anal poetry easier to bear than the national music of the same provenance. And if, for instance, Hedda Gabler,[3] a freak worthy at most of conservation in ethyl alcohol . . . well, enough. Wilbrandt and Wildenbruch's[4] most recent nonsense is even slimier.

Excuse the expectoration. I was so careless as to listen to even a part of Vierling's "Constantin."[5] Dreadfully dry, childish, pre-Mendelssohn Strauss's burlesque,[6] definitely ingenious, but on the other hand appalling, in short, this verve of rubbish and lunacy will depress and oppress me until *you*, by performing your Academic will have freed the soul[7] of your

Most loyal (pleading for protection) baton,
Bülow

No. 51

[14 January 1891]

Hamburg, 14 I 91

Esteemed Master and Friend!

B(ruckner) follows A(nton) and now that I have once begun molesting you with the Bergedorf affair, I shall have to continue with it, although now with the laudable intention of appeasement.

Returning yesterday evening from Berlin I found the following reply from Chrysander waiting for me:

"~ ~ Due to special circumstances, I have been unable to reply as of yet to your kind letter from the 8th of this year. By requesting a little more time,

I shall limit myself today to expressing my sincere and deep gratitude for your noble announcement. ~ ~

F. Chrysander"

I confess that I don't quite understand this oracle (acceptance or refusal?), perhaps my crazy head gout is at fault (chronic concert hangover).

You will have better things to do than to write me a soothing commentary, so don't bother. I shall resign to waiting and having tea,[1] the Réaumur is too low to go for a Pilsner.

In loyal devotion, your old

H v Bülow

First Class Jinx

Was Marie Soldat really born in *1846*, as Schubert's Lexicon reedited by Rabbi Breslauer says?[2]

No. 52

[17 January 1891]

Hamburg 17 I 91

Most respected Master!

Got your postscript early today. Actually, there is nothing more to say. But, on the other hand . . .

The heavenly concert report (from Friday, the 16th) by your privy councilor friend E. H.[1] has released me from such a thorough and sound depressive mood that I would like to thank him through you (nice alliteration, isn't it?) by sending the enclosed correspondence card that I received from Bergedorf yesterday. All the more, as what he says about Spitta's Bach is—as it were—emphatically anticipated by Handel's Chrysander. So that you don't waste time looking for the best part, I have taken the liberty of marking the most interesting passage with blue pencil: see page 5ff.[2]

This morning I practiced your third for the second time and I cannot spare you my confession that I'd gladly trade any one movement from it (including the third) for all of Handel's works, not to mention all the works by Couperin, Corelli, or Carissimi. The first (Couperin) in your edition[3] made me ill. I find these "Graces" worse than the style of the late père Duchêne,[4] who in *Ami du peuple* could write neither a noun without adding the decorative epithet "*fichu, foutu*" nor an adjective without "*bougrement*." Well, now I've said it. Rail if you will this odd unsaintly one, your well-known baton

Bw

May I ask you to please return Goldmann[5] at your convenience.

No. 53

[26 January 1891]

Wilhelm's Hunt* 26 I 91

Esteemed Master and dear Friend!

I'm speechless! "Having regrets"? You? Remember Grillparzer's saying, I believe found in Ottokar, "once regretted, twice erred . . ."?[1]

Well, *I* do not regret lagging behind your legislation as its executive. Proof: see the enclosures that I humbly ask be returned. Your friend, the "quaint soul" enjoyed making me sweat ink, but was ultimately clever and accepted. Please inform your esteemed friend and my gracious benefactor, too (I can't answer his amiable letter[2] (that arrived with yours) until the day after tomorrow from Hamburg). If you do wish to try out the "sudden" role: *unus poenitentium*, I fear I cannot act as your second,[3] all the less because my wife just wrote me the following:

"I just heard that yesterday (Saturday) Dr. Chrysander showed up at the North German Bank, where he, very touched and embarrassed, with qualms but also full of gratitude thanked the director (Petersen junior) so much that one has to be glad to have disposed of the money in the manner inspired by Brahms."

Chrysander's resolve to go collect the gift, so difficult to decide and yet so quickly done, shows that he really does need and has use for the money. Therefore:

Both of us may delight anew in impenitence regarding the Henry IV overture.[4] I tell you, at the prerehearsal the day before yesterday and yesterday at the final rehearsal open to the public, J. J. was as happy as the snow queen with our Schliemann[5] work (although yesterday I barked thoroughly without reason). He seemed thirty-seven years younger and played op. 59, no. 1[6] with more firework brilliance than I have seen done in a generation! Especially the scherzo made us laugh—sic!—with glee, too bad that you weren't present. Well, let's hope that this evening's audience will be at least a quarter as decent to him as recently your Alster lake dwellers were to you (Symphony III). They were literally ecstatic and wrote to all the newspapers demanding a repeat performance, as the enclosed clippings show.[7]

Life does have its bright moments. But for now I am tired of benefaction and plan, for a stimulating change, to kick out a malefactor (Bremen). All that I have done there in the past two-and-a-half years to educate the local taste in art, this disgusting careerist[8] has ruined in one year!

Fortunately for me and *you*, I've now run out of paper and time.

Most loyally, your
Bülow

No. 54

[17 February 1891]

Hamburg, 17 February 91

Esteemed Friend!

Forgive me, but I must vent my outrage at your place of residence and even your place of birth. *Vienna* sent us the nonartist, Jewish whiner D. P. (a David acting like Saul)[1] as the product of its twisted musical education and *Hamburg* applauded him frenetically. Ugh! To the devil with the Hellmesberg[2] school of coquetry and dirt. Haydn's cello concerto itself is worth burying, but the way this charlatan caricatured and painted it with filth—well, the source of the theme for your opuses 56 a & b certainly didn't deserve that!

I felt just the same way you did the first time you heard Victor Nessler.

Anyway, in the end he did your Academic [Overture] a favor that was performed and received with an enthusiasm unknown of all around Bergedorf. A few evenings ago Miss Barbi[3] sang two songs of yours in the same place, more beautiful than anything else and much, much warmer than pretty Hermine[4] ever could.

So, now I have cooled off a little.

The drawback of a good memory is a bad conscience. Recently I misquoted Grillparzer[5] for you. It should read:

> To regret one's deeds is to err twice: first for doing it, then for regretting it.
> (*A loyal servant of the Lord*).

This being a favorable occasion, let me also cite the following from Grillparzer's diary (Paris, Wednesday 13 April 1836):

"Incidentally, Germans of all kinds are the same. You have to have a particularly cordial relationship with them not to find them insipid."

Did the cordiality of my letter to E. H.[6] spare me being found insipid?

By the way, the citation above reminded me of Bergedorf. Through the intervention of third parties, I *finally* got him [Chrysander] to reword a note on how he plans to use the sum awarded him. Though I don't like the phrasing, it will be printed uncensored in the Friedrichsruh (alias Hamburg) newspaper[7] as it must; at least this finally gets it off my desk. Although it will hardly interest you, I will send our un-Philistine honorary citizen a copy.

From the habitually bad tone of these lines you will perhaps conclude that my ass health (don't take that physiologically) has improved somewhat. Indeed, thanks to my illustrious friend from Bologna,[8] after two weeks the electricity is working.

"Our favorites" (Reinecke[9]), a) the son of the mayor of Graz has a colossal inability to conduct and was fired immediately[10] (he knocked over the water carrier, excusing himself by saying that "he was unfamiliar with it") and b) little Fritz from Rotterdam was enthusiastically rejected in Frankfurt.[11] But

❀ **Concerthaus — Conventgarten.** ❀

Montag den 16. Februar 1891, Abends 7½ Uhr pünktlich

IX. ABONNEMENT-CONCERT

Dirigent: Dr. Hans von Bülow.

Solisten: { David Popper *(Cello).*
{ Franz Schwarz *(Bariton).*

PROGRAMM.

1. „Von der Nordsee", Sinfonie D moll,
   op. 4 (neu, Manuscript) . . . . . . *F. E. Koch.*
   a) Friesenfahrt. Leidenschaftlich bewegt.
   b) Sommerabend am Strande. Langsam.
   c) Spiel der Wellen. Nicht schnell, mit Humor.
      Anmuthig, tändelnd.
   d) Auf hoher See. Breit und wuchtig. Stürmisch
      bewegt.

2. Ouverture zur Oper „Iphigenie in Aulis"
   (1774) mit dem Schlusse von Rich.
   Wagner (1861) . . . . *Gluck.*
3. Scene und Arie aus der Oper „Iphigenie
   in Aulis" . . . . *Gluck.*
      Herr Franz Schwarz.
4. Concert für Violoncell . . . . . *Haydn.*
      Herr David Popper.
5. Nachtstück. . . . . *F. Schubert.*
      Herr Franz Schwarz.
6. Cellosoli.
      a) Träumerei . . . . *R. Schumann.*
      b) Spinnerlied . . . . *D. Popper.*
      Herr David Popper.
      Klavierbegleitung: Herr **William Sichel.**
7. Akademische Festouverture, op. 80 . . *J. Brahms.*
   wirkte erlösend! ✻✻✻

X. (Letztes) Abonnement-Concert: Montag den 2. März 1891.

Schumann: Ouverture „Braut von Messina". — **Schumann:** Klavierconcert
A moll. — **Joachim:** Ouverture „Heinrich IV." (Manuscript). — Klaviersolo.
Liszt: Spanische Rhapsodie. — **Beethoven:** Sinfonie No. VIII.
Solist: Eugen d'Albert.

Enclosure to Letter No. 54. *Staatsbibliothek zu Berlin—Preussischer Kulturbesitz; SBB Mus. Ep. Hans von Bülow 333*

you know that. I did what I could for Kirchner, but . . . it won't work. I *must* transcribe Bungert's lieder for Luckhardt![12] Farewell, write soon to
Your most loyal artistic servant
Bülow

[Enclosure: Printed program. Under the last item, the Academic Festival Overture, Bülow wrote, "most redeeming!"]

No. 55

[17 February 1892]

Hamburg 17 II 92

Esteemed Master and Friend!

A little letter from Hans Brahms—oh—one must say thank-you right away! Yes (what a relief!), I'm up and running again, as you and I see. You'd never guess which new chance doctor (med.) made it happen. If I were to tell you, you'd think I'm a lying journalist. But it's true.

At the mayor's festive dinner on 16 January—attached is the gastronomical concert program (for a change), well . . . guess what? None other, by J.!, than your equally highborn, co-honorary citizen from Friedrichsruh[1] [revealed to me] by a kiss on my right cheek (so sacred to me [since *you* kissed it]) that the day after tomorrow, by the time you have received these lines, I will have taken the oath as a citizen of Hamburg.

Berlin 92/93—never. Here are my reasons (formed by decent foes, not by friendly blockheads). *Your cult,* my dear friend, is secured by making Rafael Maszkowski[2] from Breslau my successor. The paragons of both virtue and evil trust him just as much as I mistrust them. Therefore . . . and so on.

If I should still be waving the baton in '93, well, I could return to help enforce the principles of '93 that currently seem to be more opportune for our country than those of '89.[3]

For a while I have been doing what I can for your old paramour Theodora,[4] not without success. "I feel so horribly *super*fluous" she recently sighed again. I got gruff and barked:[5] *Then get fluid* [solvent]*!*[6] She[7] nodded, seeming to get the point. (Isn't that how Kalbeck puts it?)[8] When will you be coming here with Emmy to become godparents for Johannes Joseph Julius?[9] Please inform your

Most loyal, devoted
Bw

10th Concert in Berlin, 28 March, same as on the 21st:

Bach B minor Suite
Brahms A major Serenade
Beethoven Eroica

Decent ending? Well . . . ?[10]

No. 56

[6 April 1892]

Berlin, 6 April 1892

Esteemed Master!
Dear Friend!

Black? My *favorite* relative, President von Bojanowski,[1] my sister's husband, died eight days ago of the flu.

Otherwise, things are as *rosy* as Bismarck's cheeks on his 77th birthday.

I have conquered the bastion of both the press and the audience at once.[2] It was such a wonderful moment that now the lemures may come and get me.[3] But then again, I would rather they didn't. You know what a pleasure it is to perform your Serenade in A major *six times* in two weeks (half in Hamburg and half here) with *deserved* great success.[4] Well, even if you had less desire than time for it, do please make an exception and share the joy, particularly for Fritz (*amico-editore*)![5]

After a short stay in Munich (Lenbach),[6] on April 10th we will be steaming off to Italy for five weeks. From there I would like to congratulate you on May 7th by telegram—where will you be? Would you approve of Berlioz's *Faust* as a modest token of my devotion?[7]

Most deeply, loyally, and always your
Bülow[8]

No. 57

[1 August 1892]

Hamburg, 1 August 92

Esteemed Master, revered Friend!

No month can begin more "augustly" than by getting greetings from you. My most heartfelt thanks! Of course I will grab the opportunity with all ten fingers and ask you to send me your kindly offered test booklet[1] straightaway. If I should discover a suitable piece, I'll copy it and immediately return your manuscript or the copy you send me. By the end of the week I'll be "soaking up" sea air (Skodsborg near Copenhagen or someplace similar). But I'll be finished with that in three or four weeks, leaving twenty-five days in September to still sweat at the piano.

You will join in, won't you, in my unconditional self-praise for always preserving the decorum of the most proper discretion toward you during the quarter of a century of our intercourse? From various sides I had heard that you recently made posthumous competition for Couperin, but I manfully suppressed the urge to ask out of curiosity. I also feared that . . . considering the difference in glove size between Joachim's beard[2] and my nothingness . . . well, it's not worth completing the sentence.

Nonetheless, for the sake of rarity, I shall be so bold as to bother you. I've been thinking of slowly but surely convincing the citizens of Hamburg to overcome their reservations and erect a monument to Heinrich Heine on Jungfernstieg [Street] near the Alster pavilion, just where the poet told his worst jokes about them. As an appropriate fanfare, as soon as possible Böhme could publish a lieder album with proceeds going to the H. H. fund. You certainly have an old Heine lied among your "Valses oubliées," don't you? The important thing is your name. Would you like to give us or him that gift? Or do you disapprove of the enterprise? I can't believe that. On the contrary, I optimistically claim the opposite. *So, then* . . . *???*[3]

Recently Hamburg's senate, despite its lingering headlessness (two or more months ago mayor Petersen became perilously ill, but has been recovering over the past two weeks), exhibited a very laudable sign of dignity. The Capri-critters[4] had officially proposed to punish Bismarck's local spokesman, the "[Hamburg] News," for its loyalty by withdrawing *all official public announcements*. Isn't that *outrageous*? Well, anyway, our *patres concripti* turned the proposal down courteously, but coldly.

But now I have forgotten myself, I mean, your lack of pedantry for the written word. Farewell, fare most heavenly!

Always your most loyal artistic servant,
Bülow[5]

COMMENTARY

Legend

> ep. = *epistula* (letter)
> r = *recto* (front side)
> v = *verso* (back side)

Letter No. 1

Sign.: Mus. ep. Hans von Bülow 281. One double page, written on one side (1r) only.

1. Fritz Simrock (1838–1901) owned a music publishing company founded ca. 1790 by Nikolaus Simrock in Bonn. In 1870 he moved the

business to Berlin. Brahms and Simrock had met in 1860. Thereafter most of Brahms's works were published by Simrock. After becoming acquainted with Symphony no. 1, op. 68, in September in Baden-Baden, Bülow wished to perform it in the late fall during his already scheduled concert tour through Scotland (cf. letter no. 2, note 3). (It did happen on 17 December 1877 in Edinburgh.) Brahms had already agreed to the idea orally and also asked Simrock to have the material prepared by the end of November (letter dated 27 Sept. 1877; cf. BBW X/2, p. 48). Bülow's idea to perform the symphony sooner, before leaving for Britain, in his new position in Hanover, complicated things because the symphony's parts and score were not to appear in print until late October. Proofreading had not been completed at the time Bülow wrote his letter. Bülow had his superior, Bronsart (see note 2), ask Simrock to send him the galley proofs to rehearse the concert. We know this from Simrock's letter to Brahms dated 28 Sept. 1877: "Hanover has asked me to send special copies to Bülow, too. I can't be sending extra copies all over the place. He'll get them at October's end—that's early enough, isn't it?" Kurt Stephenson, *Johannes Brahms und Fritz Simrock: Weg einer Freundschaft* (Hamburg, 1961), p. 108. Having pointed out the official date of publication, Simrock considered the issue settled; he did not reply to Bülow or Bronsart.

2. As of 1867 the director of the royal theater at "Welfenheim" (home of the ducal family the Guelphs = Hanover) was Hans Bronsart von Schellendorf (1830–1913), who like Bülow had been one of Liszt's pupils. In mid-August 1877 the sudden death of the orchestra's lead conductor Karl Ludwig Fischer (1816–1877) had left the position vacant, and Bronsart did not hesitate to offer it to his longtime friend, Hans von Bülow. Bülow, who found himself in a severe medical and emotional crisis following his first and exhausting concert tour of the United States (in May 1876) took up the position by directing the orchestra's first subscription concert on 19 September 1877. After leaving Munich, it gave him the first opportunity to work on a long-term basis with an orchestra, and he stayed there until the autumn of 1879.

3. Bülow called Brahms's First Symphony in C major op. 68, "Beethoven's Tenth." This later famous bon mot soon became public when Bülow wrote travel reviews for several issues of the journal *Signale für die musikalische Welt* (vol. 35, nos. 61, 62, and 64 [1877]), which later were again issued as reprints. He had used the phrase in passing in a dispute with Max Bruch, writing (in *Signale*, 1877, no. 62) [= third November issue, dated 27 Oct.–4 Nov. 1877, p. 980], "It was not until I became acquainted with the *tenth symphony*, alias Johannes Brahms's first symphony, in other words, not until six weeks ago, that I lost favor and patience with Bruch's fragments★ and such things. I call it the *tenth* not because it ranks after the "ninth": actually I would position it between the second and *Eroica* . . . ." Ten years later Bülow gave his

expression of the relation between Brahms's and Beethoven's symphonies a somewhat different twist. This had to do with an aversion he developed late in life to the final movement of Beethoven's Ninth Symphony. In a letter to Bronsart dated 3 August 1888, he wrote that "naturally Brahms did not write *the tenth Beethoven symphony*, but unfortunately also not the finale for the 'ninth' which he could have done to the greater honor of its first three movements" (BBS VII [7], p. 205).

★A pun on Bruch-Stücke [Bruch's pieces] and Bruchstücke [fragments]. CK

4. On 4 November 1876, Otto Dessoff (1835–1892; court conductor in Karlsruhe from 1875 to 1881) had conducted the première of Brahms's First Symphony in Karlsruhe; Brahms was present.

5. Brahms complied with Bülow's request to intervene on his behalf, writing on 5 October 1877 to Simrock:

> *Dear Simrock!*
>
> *Bülow (at Rudolph's Hotel in Hanover) wishes so sincerely to perform our symphony on the twentieth of this month in Hanover and I wish even more to do him this favor. He is really so pleased with the piece that I ask you kindly to do what can be done. A couple of mistakes won't ruin the performance! At any rate, please do pen him a few words—for the worst case I have already informed him how much trouble you have had with such requests in the past. However, I do feel that Bülow especially deserves it—I hope it works?! (BBW X, p. 50)*

Brahms also sent a reply to Bülow on the same day, mentioning his letter to Simrock, but doubting whether the endeavor would be successful (because Simrock shunned such special favors in order to spare himself similar print-interrupting requests). Alluding to the September days in Baden-Baden, when he had demonstrated to Bülow his own interpretation of the first symphony on the piano, Brahms continues in the same letter:

> *I'm sorry that recently I did not continue chatting at the piano. Dessoff says of another first movement that I played for him that I have never yet written anything so lovely. [Brahms means the second symphony, with which Bülow is not yet familiar.] Now I can expect that all the critics who didn't like the first one will say of the second (and others to come) that the composer was unable to match the quality of his first try. And meanwhile number this or that is one of the greatest works of its kind, and that in the past decades nothing so significant has been written on Lake Wörth since Volkmann's third, Raff's thirteenth, Kiel's first. (Kalbeck 3/2, p. 232)*

Letter No. 2

Sign.: Mus. ep. Hans von Bülow 282. One double page, written on two sides (1r+2r).

1. Bülow had sent the telegram to Simrock *réponse payee*. Simrock, to whom Brahms had written on 5 October, hesitated to reply immediately because at Brahms's request he had ordered copies for Hanover from printer Röder in Leipzig and was waiting for them. Finally, when the packet from Leipzig took too long, on the evening of 15 October, Simrock wired back to Bülow: "Waited in vain for the copies, thus my belated reply, letter will follow." Kurt Stephenson, *Johannes Brahms und Fritz Simrock: Weg einer Freundschaft* (Hamburg, 1961), p. 110.

2. A startled Simrock informed Brahms of Bülow's telegram (Stephenson, p. 109; the date provided there is incorrect). This prompted Brahms to confide frankly to Simrock:

> *Bülow cannot keep his witticisms and thoughts to himself. I hope this time he has learned from it, but we shall see. I think and have thought about writing to him, but the matter seems so obvious that I don't think he needs my reprimanding. I regret being the cause of all this and my only consolation is that I enabled both him and you to say no. (BBW X, p. 51f.)*

3. The copies arrived just in time for Simrock to send them off late in the evening of 15 October after all. Thus, contrary to Bülow's fears, the First Symphony could be performed on 20 October 1877 as the third concert in the subscription series.

4. Prior to concluding his engagement in Hanover, Bülow had obligated himself to conduct orchestral concerts in Glasgow and Edinburgh at the beginning of the winter season. To do so he was granted leave from the end of October 1877 until mid-January 1878, in other words for the period between the third (20 Oct. 1877) and fourth (19 Jan. 1877) subscription concerts.

Letter No. 3

Sign.: Mus. ep. Hans von Bülow 283. One double page, written on two sides (1r+2r).

1. After Bülow resigned from his conducting position in Hanover (petition for release dated 26 Oct. 1879), Duke George II from Saxe-Meiningen immediately asked him to conduct the ducal court orchestra there in a position created just for Bülow. The decree is from 10 February 1880. Taking up the position in the autumn of 1880, Bülow lived at the Hotel "Saxon Court"; he did not move into an apartment of his own until 10 October 1881.

2. Brahms's letter from July 1881 reads,

Dearest Baron and Esteemed Colleague,

I must take a few words to tell you that I currently think often of you and your friendly suggestion to sometime have a thorough rehearsal in Meiningen. The occasion presents itself, but it is a piano concerto that could use such rehearsal! Besides my other modest concerns, I shy considerably from sight-reading such a piece in your presence.

You are a little familiar with my somewhat special relationship to the piano and with me as a pianist, above all you are aware of my great respect for you!

But I write these lines to keep that [great respect] from tempting me to pass up your wonderful offer and to go forward with the next subscription concert. The simplest solution would be for you to say that a piano concerto is not what we had discussed and not what you have in mind!

My address is Pressbaum near Vienna.

In cordial esteem,
Your loyal J. Brahms

(BBS VII [6], p. 80)

During a conversation in Vienna in February 1881, Bülow had suggested to Brahms that he come to Meiningen and try out his compositions with the orchestra far from the attention of the greater public (Kalbeck 3/2, p. 306). At the time Bülow was in Vienna giving concerts: On 10 February he played Beethoven's last five piano sonatas, on 20 February he played Beethoven's Fourth Piano Concerto with the Vienna Philharmonic (directed by Hans Richter), and on 21 February he gave a Liszt soirée in the Bösendorfer salon that Brahms attended.

3. These original plans were altered, and between 1 and 21 January 1882, the Meiningen Court Orchestra gave Brahms concerts in the following cities: two evening concerts in Berlin (8 and 9 Jan.), one in Kiel (12 Jan.), one in Hamburg (15 Jan.). Except for one Mendelssohn soirée in Berlin (7 Jan.), all of the other performances were purely Beethoven concerts. The overall itinerary was as follows: 1 Jan., Eisenach; 4 to 9 Jan. (daily concerts), Berlin; 10 and 11 Jan., Hamburg; 12 and 13 Jan., Kiel; 14 Jan., Bremen; 15 Jan., Hamburg; 16 to 18 Jan., Berlin; 19 Jan., Halberstadt; 20 Jan., Leipzig; and 21 Jan., Köthen.

Letter No. 4

Sign.: Mus. ep. Hans von Bülow 284. One double page, written on two sides (1r+2r), printed letterhead: "Director of the Ducal Court Orchestra, Meiningen the . . . 18—."

1. The item has not survived. The program in Meiningen for the season of 1881 included six subscription concerts (30 Oct., 6 Nov., 13 Nov., 27

Nov., 4 Dec., and 11 Dec.) and two benefit concerts for the court orchestra's widow and orphan fund (20 Nov. and 26 Dec.).

Letter No. 5

Sign.: Mus. ep. Hans von Bülow 285. One double page, written on two sides (1r+2r), the last line written as a postscript on 1v [lengthwise].

1. The note appearing in the daily newspaper *Berliner Tageblatt* read, "Soon Brahms will be traveling to Meiningen to Hans von Bülow for the purpose of studying his own, second piano concerto with the latter." The line had been reprinted from a similar announcement that had appeared beforehand in the journal *Musikwelt* (Kalbeck 3/2, p. 311).

2. Bülow placed a corrective statement in the *Berliner Tageblatt* of 13 January:

> Dr. Brahms has kindly consented to the undersigned to give the court orchestra under the direction of the undersigned the honor of revising and correcting its studies of his symphonic works and during his visit, scheduled for the seventeenth of this month, to try his new piano concerto (in manuscript) for the first time in the accompaniment of an orchestra. *We* are the ones that will be *studying*. (Kalbeck 3/2, p. 311)

Letter No. 6

Sign.: Mus. ep. Hans von Bülow 286. One double page, written on two sides (1r+2r).

1. Duke George II of Saxe-Meiningen (1826–1914; accession to power on 20 Sept. 1866) married in 1873 his third wife, Helene Baroness of Heldburg (1839–1923), the actress Ellen Franz, upon whom he bestowed the title of nobility.

2. [Brahms dedicated this dirge to Henriette Feuerbach at the loss of her son, painter Anselm Feuerbach.]

3. Printing was not yet completed, and the orchestral parts arrived in Meiningen a few at a time, as they became ready. The string parts arrived a day after this letter was written, on 14 October (cf. BBW XVII, p. 21, note 2). The score was not published until July 1882. In Meiningen the musicians played from the manuscript.

4. The enclosure has not survived. It was a telegraphic inquiry from Henriette Fritsch-Estrangin (cf. letter no. 16, note 4), apparently in reaction to the newspaper announcement mentioned in letter no. 5, note 1.

5. August Walter (1821–1896), music instructor and director in Basel as of 1846. The incident Bülow mentions relates to Brahms's stay in Basel (in

early November 1866, not in 1867) during his concert tour to Switzerland and Alsace with Joseph Joachim from 20 October to 10 November 1866.

6. Cellist Friedrich Hilpert (1841–1896) was a member of the Meiningen Court Orchestra from 1876 to 1885. The mixed choir he directed had been established at Bülow's initiative one month before Bülow took up practical work in Meiningen.

7. The *Deutsches Requiem* (German Requiem), op. 45, was performed on 20 November 1881 as part of a benefit concert for the court orchestra's widows and orphans fund (the second half of the program was Beethoven's Symphony no. 5). Brahms, whom Bülow had "implored" *not* to attend (see above), did not arrive in Meiningen until 24 November.

Letter No. 7

Sign.: Mus. ep. Hans von Bülow 287. One double page, written on one side (1r).

1. Marie von Bülow's edition of the letters (BBS VII [6], p. 98) dates this one as being from 15 October, which would have been prior to Brahms's visit from 17 to 22 [?] October. But the somewhat illegible date is clearly Oct. 25. We also know from a letter that Bülow wrote to Hermann Wolff, dated 27 October 1881 (BBS VII [6], p. 99), that the "poor health" mentioned in closing the letter developed shortly before Brahms left Meiningen.

2. Brahms did actually direct Symphony no. 1 himself. The selections and order of the program for 27 November, however, underwent several changes (see letter no. 9, note 2). In his reply, Brahms did not take up Bülow's suggestion. Instead, he wrote,

After the amusing piece, any audience will take a little abuse. Just recently in Pest I saw how gladly the orchestra and the audience jumped for 6/8! . . . Really, leave things the way they are, don't make the overture sound like a feeble da capo of the finale. (Quoted from BBS VII [6], p. 104f., footnote 1)

Letter No. 8

Sign.: Mus. ep. Hans von Bülow 288. One double page, written on one side (1r).

1. Max Abbass (1844–1923), member of the Meiningen Court Orchestra and first flute as of 1873. From 1876 to 1911 he managed the orchestra's library.

2. See letter no. 10, note 4.

Letter No. 9

Sign.: Mus. ep. Hans von Bülow 289. One double page, written on one side (1r).

1. Regarding this invitation by the duke (telegram dated 16 Nov. 1881) see BBW XVII, p. 22. Brahms stayed in Meiningen from 24 to 30 November 1881.

2. Brahms did not agree with Bülow's plan. A preview notice included in the program for the concert given on 20 November (cf. letter no. 6, note 6) said the program for 27 November would be as follows: Tragic Overture op. 81; Academic Festival Overture op. 80; Piano Concerto no. 2, op. 83; Symphony no. 1, op. 68. However, at the actual subscription concert on 27 November, the pieces were performed in this order: Tragic Overture op. 81; Piano Concerto no. 2, op. 83 (solo: Brahms); Haydn Variations op. 56a; Academic Festival Overture op. 80; Symphony no. 1, op. 68 (the two last pieces directed by Brahms).

★ A pun combining the word *unpässlich* (ailing) and Bülow's neologism *unbässlich* (lacking a contrabass).

Letter No. 10

Sign.: Mus. ep. Hans von Bülow 290. One double page, written on two sides (1r+2r).

★ A play on the name of the town Meiningen and the possessives *mein* (my) and *dein* (your): *Meiningen-Deinigen* = My town, your town.

★★ After the first of two Brahms concerts in Berlin on 8 January (Bülow's birthday), Brahms conferred on Bülow the honor of using the German personal address *Du*.

★★★ Take the train.

1. Bülow's first piano soirée including exclusively works by Brahms took place on 2 February 1882 in Vienna as the first in a series of three piano concerts (the other two were mixed programs on 8 and 14 February). The Brahms evening included Piano Sonata no. 2, op. 2; Variations op. 21b; Rhapsodies op. 79; Piano Pieces op. 76; ballades from op. 10; Scherzo op. 4; and Handel Variations op. 24.

2. Max Kalbeck (1850–1921), music critic and writer, later Brahms's biographer, was a music critic for the *Wiener Allgemeine Zeitung* from 1880 to 1883 and then a music critic for the *Presse*. He was extraordinarily skeptical of Bülow and mistrusted the latter's newfound enthusiasm for Brahms. This

is clearly mirrored in his review of Bülow's Brahms soirée mentioned in note 1 above:

> Bülow, who was more nervous and played less calmly than last winter, did not trust all the applause and tried to escape by playfully threatening the audience. Recalled again and again he warned: "My dears, if you do not cease clapping I'll play the last fugue [from op. 24] again." Can one be more indiscreet in blurting out one's most hidden thoughts? (*Wiener Allgemeine Zeitung*, 4 February 1882)

3. The concert in Leipzig on 20 January 1882 (as part of the Meiningen orchestra's tour from 1 to 21 January 1882) consisted purely of Beethoven pieces: Leonore Overture no. 3; Symphony no. 1, op. 21; Overture from "King Stephan"; and Symphony no. 3, op. 55 (the *Eroica*).

4. Edmund Koch, attendant for the Meiningen Court Orchestra as of 1879. During Brahms's stay in Berlin (for concerts on 7 and 8 January), Simrock lent Brahms a frock coat [German: *Rock*] because Brahms had (purposely) not prepared his wardrobe for the social obligations tied to the concerts (cf. Brahms's letter to Simrock prior to his arrival in Berlin, BBW X, p. 197).

5. Lessmann had a "correction" printed in the paper. It read,

> The last number of this paper contained a brief note on the most recent philharmonic concert [in Hamburg] that demands slight revision. . . . I *definitely* object to the claim that the concert was obscure or even uncomely for the following reason: It is entirely impossible to *judge* a large and significant work after hearing it once or twice. . . . Incidentally, I must admit that I found much of the concert delightful, for instance, the final movement, as well as the beginning of the first movement with its sonorous horn motif, and how masterly was the arrangement for piano and orchestra! Neither do I understand how anyone can say that Brahms has never been an important virtuoso, that he *significantly* lacks technique and confidence, or that he has a *hard, unmusical touch*. (*ADMZ* 9, no. 3 [20 Jan. 1882]: p. 27, signed: E. Schweitzer)

For Bülow it was not enough to notify Brahms that the claims had been revoked; he saw to it that a copy of the paper was delivered to Brahms. In an unpublished letter from Bülow to Lessmann (Meiningen, 23 Jan. 1882) we read,

> Among many other things, thank you sincerely for rectifying in your most recent number the appraisal of Brahms in Hamburg. . . . Please be sure to send a copy to Brahms (addressed to Prof. Engelmann in Utrecht). Mark it in blue to make sure he reads it. The previous issue upset him. (SBB, Sign.: Mus. Ep. Hans von Bülow 232)

6. Otto Lessmann (1844–1918) was editor of the *Allgemeine Deutsche Musik-Zeitung* (*ADMZ*) from 1881 to 1907. Lessmann had been a student of piano at Bülow's Stern Conservatory. In 1882 he persuaded Bülow to write a few articles for the paper.

7. The *Allgemeine Deutsche Musik-Zeitung* (vol. 9, no. 2 [dated 13 January 1882]: p. 19) had reprinted the following anonymous correspondent's note from Hamburg about the Hamburg Philharmonic Concert of 6 January 1882, where Brahms had played Piano Concerto no. 2:

> Less fortunate was the four movement-long, often very murky (if not to say ugly) concerto that certainly could not prove its worth because it was performed so poorly. As far as I know, Brahms has never been an important virtuoso, but besides a significant lack of technique and aplomb, he also has a hard, unmusical touch that constantly hurt my ears. The most beautiful cantilena sounded stiff and in order to evaluate the composition, that is definitely grand, I wish to hear it played by an important pianist.

8. The *Signale für die musikalische Welt* [Signals for the World of Music] (vol. 40, no. 3 [third issue in January 1882]: p. 34) printed the following lines (by Eduard Bernsdorf) about the eleventh subscription concert in Leipzig's Gewandhaus Hall on 1 January 1882, where Brahms had played both Rhapsodies op. 79 and the Piano Concerto no. 2, op. 83: "Compared to the first concerto the second seems to have only negative advantages: it is less ugly and less tasteless, less abstruse and less obscure, it is overall less unhealthy and less unnatural." The writer upbraids the work for being "enormously long," without sufficiently compensating the hearer with "anything fascinating or attractive, anything satisfying in form or content, or anything free of tediousness or stolidness." The report ends with a critique of "Brahms's piano talent . . . , that in both the concerto and the two rhapsodies did indeed not lack all sorts of critical elements." The "exemplary punishment" that Bülow announced he would bestow upon the music world of Leipzig took place on 14 March 1882, the next time the Meiningen Court Orchestra played in Leipzig, where Bülow gave the audience a piece of his mind (see note 10 below).

9. During his first visit to Meiningen (in October 1881), George II had awarded Brahms the *Komturkreuz*, a medal of distinction. [Bülow makes a pun of *Com*thur and *com*poser. CK]

10. In mid-March the Meiningen Court Orchestra gave three concerts in Leipzig's Gewandhaus Hall: on 13 March 1882 a concert with exclusively Beethoven works, on 14 March 1882 a purely Brahms program (without Brahms, unfortunately for Bülow), and on 17 March 1882 a Mendelssohn-Schumann soirée. The program for the Brahms evening (deviating slightly from the previously mentioned program in Hamburg from 15 January 1882,

which also included the Academic Festival Overture op. 80) read, Piano Concerto no. 1, op. 15 (solo: Bülow, directed by Bülow's substitute conductor Mannstädt); Haydn Variations op. 56a; Symphony op. 68. On this occasion Bülow gave one of his infamous speeches that in this case could only be understood against the background of his fury over the Leipzig concert review that had appeared in January of the same year (see note 8 above). The audience either could not or would not see any connection and reacted with estrangement. On 16 March 1882 the *Leipziger Tageblatt* printed Bülow's words: "I thank you for your concern, not only in my name, but also in the name of His Highness the Duke of Saxe-Meiningen, who has sent us here *to gratify Master Johannes Brahms for* [the damage done on] *the first of January*." The writer adds the following typical comment: "We regret endlessly that yesterday's celebration of Brahms was later so ruined by trying to make us see it as an act of reparation." Another version of Bülow's address to the audience, worded slightly differently, but having the same content, can be found in Bernard Vogel, *Hans von Bülow: Sein Leben und Sein Entwicklungsgang* (Leipzig, 1887), p. 40.

11. Elisabeth von Herzogenberg, née von Stockhausen (1847–1892), to whom Brahms dedicated the Rhapsodies op. 79, had temporarily been one of his piano pupils in Vienna. As of 1872 she lived in Leipzig, and she was present at Bülow's concert on 20 January. From her correspondence with Brahms we know that while Brahms was interested in the March Leipzig concerts that Bülow had announced (although he preferred to come and listen, not to participate) and that he had arranged to visit the Herzogenberg family on 17 March (in other words, too late), he eventually did not journey to Leipzig at all because Bülow had left him uninformed of the final plans (BBW I, p. 171). A day after the concert, Elisabeth von Herzogenberg wrote to Brahms (15 March 1882), "Obviously Bülow was very happy yesterday, but also very disappointed that you did not come. We did not tell him it was his own fault, in order not to agitate him before the concert" (BBW I, p. 174).

[Bülow's nickname "dedi-kitten" for Elisabeth von Herzogenberg is a pun on dedi-*cat*-ion. CK]

12. *Res severa verum gaudium* was the motto over the entrance of the Leipzig Gewandhaus. Originally from Lucius Annaeus Seneca's (4 BC–AD 65) *Epistulae morales ad Lucilium* (no. 23): *Mihi crede, res severa est verum gaudium.*

13. Pun on the name Schiedam, a harbor city bordering Rotterdam [and the German colloquialism "*auf dem Damme sein*" = to feel up to it (literally, to be on the dam) CK]. Brahms spent the last ten days of January in Holland, playing his Piano Concerto no. 2, op. 83, in several cities.

14. Kalbeck (3/2, p. 309) wrote of Brahms's reply to Bülow's news that he had conquered Leipzig: Brahms "hopes to still find him sacking the (momentarily not overly inaccessible) terrain." In reply to Bülow's promise to

hand over to him the [music] keys [of the city], Brahms wrote, "*The metaphor doesn't suit Leipzig—but if you want to cathartically storm through the place again, I'd be glad to join you.*"

No. 11 (Telegram)

Sign.: Mus. ep. Hans von Bülow Varia 6. Standard telegram form. The post-mark from Vienna indicates that it was submitted at 9:55 o'clock.

1. In the spring of 1882 Bülow was on a concert tour through Scandinavia. The seventh of May is Brahms's birthday.

Letter No. 12

Sign.: Mus. ep. Hans von Bülow 291. One double page, written on four sides (1r+v, 2r+v), on the upper left the paper bears a Brahms portrait in half profile.

1. Brahms had written on letter paper displaying a Bülow portrait. For his reply, Bülow used, for the first time, letter paper displaying a Brahms portrait at the top. Brahms had not heard about Bülow's engagement directly from Bülow, but having heard a rumor, he inquired in Meiningen (letter dated 1 May 1882 to George II; cf. BBW XVII, p. 25) and then wrote to Bülow, thanking him for the telegram from May 7:

> *Dear Friend,*
>
> *I should have thanked you long ago for your congratulations of May 7 and sent you congratulations myself. But I never really know just where you are, nor whether this time people are telling the truth. Apparently they are, so I do want to cordially give you my best wishes. To make them sound sincere, I should provide some sort of proof and follow your example!* [marry] *But I cannot, because one does have principles, and I set myself one long ago. Yet it is sad that one does not learn young enough and believe that zeros multiply* [income will happen] *and one unintentionally and effortlessly, unfortunately without a purpose, becomes a capitalist!*
>
> *You have a more fortunate disposition than I. You take pleasure in so many things and do them with such earnestness—while I do almost the contrary.*
>
> *I've been here in Ischl now for about eight days; as of yesterday I'm a summer guest because the day before we still had wonderful snow flurries. You will be preparing for Aachen and can be proud that you've gotten such an ill-famed piece as the D minor concerto accepted for a music festival!*
>
> *Should I happen—or not—to send you some lieder booklets—don't resent it. I don't yet know whether I'm too embarrassed, or whether I can expect the groom to put up with a little gentle sentimentality.*
>
> *Now commend me to your bride as best you can, in other words, show her a picture of me that is twenty years old, and don't play any sonatas in F-sharp minor to her, play her an intermezzo in A-flat major—you do that very well.*

When you get to Aachen greet my friend Wüllner cordially. Hopefully the music and bustle there will do him good after what he's been through. Actually, I should be at Lake Como and I fear that your esteemed and beloved parties will be unable to think and understand some things—and thus resent them!

Now, forgive me all this chitchat. Your bride may begin below and read just the good part from the bottom up!

Entirely and cordially, your loyal
J. Brahms

(Taken from Kalbeck 3/2, p. 347f.)

The last sentence refers to Bülow's portrait at the bottom of the stationery that Brahms used upside down.

2. At the 35th Lower Rhine Music Festival in Aachen (31 May to 2 June 1857) Bülow had performed Liszt's Piano Concerto no. 1 in E-flat major (under Liszt's supervision). He was scheduled to participate on 30 May 1882 in the 59th Lower Rhine Music Festival in Aachen (25 to 30 May) to perform Brahms's Piano Concerto no. 1, op. 15.

3. Ferdinand (von) Hiller (1811–1885), as of 1850 municipal orchestra director of Cologne, director of the Concert Society, the Concert Choir, and director of the Cologne Conservatory. Once it was over, Hiller wrote several articles on the 35th Lower Rhine Music Festival (1857) for the *Kölnische Zeitung* (Cologne Newspaper). These were all the more embarrassing for Bülow because they combined praise for his talent at the piano with harsh criticism of his teacher Liszt as a conductor; the critiques were so harsh that even Liszt's opponents found them abhorrent.

4. In the autumn of 1877 Bülow had met actress Marie Schanzer (1857–1941) in Karlsruhe, where she played the part of Minna of Barnhelm at the court theater. Afterward he tried (unsuccessfully, but that was not Bronsart's fault) to get her work in Hanover, where he conducted. Their first personal encounter occurred when she came to Hanover for a guest performance. After having met again on 15 January 1882 in Hamburg, Bülow was able to arrange for her to act in Meiningen (cf. BBS VII, p. 132); as of February 1882 she belonged to the troupe of Meiningen court actors. The marriage ceremony did not, as suggested in the letter, take place in August like his marriage to Cosima (18 August 1857). Bülow married Marie Schanzer on 29 July 1882.

5. The program for the Brahms matinee on 15 January 1882 in Hamburg's city theater was as follows: Piano Concerto no. 1, op. 15 (solo: Bülow, conducted by Brahms); Haydn Variations op. 56a (conducted by Bülow); Academic Festival Overture (conducted by Brahms); Symphony no. 1, op. 68 (conducted by Bülow).

6. In April 1881 Bülow saw his daughter Daniela (1860–1940) for the first time in twelve years. Unlike her younger sister Blandine (1863–1941),

after this reencounter Daniela developed a close, confidential relationship to Bülow.

Bülow wanted to combine a viewing of *Parsifal* with his attendance at Blandine's marriage (to Count Biagio Gravina). But before mid-May Daniela had written him that Cosima wished otherwise (*New Letters*, p. 587). Upon this, Bülow wrote Daniela that he would visit her incognito (except to her) during his performance tour in August (*New Letters*, p. 588f.). He did not meet his daughter Blandine again until 1884, after a separation of fifteen years, when she—at his invitation—visited him with her spouse in Meiningen.

7. Violinist and composer Joseph Joachim (1831–1907) was concertmaster in Weimar from 1849 to 1853, under the direction of Franz Liszt, and then became the same in Hanover. As of 1853 he was close friends with Brahms. In Weimar, Bülow had already joined Joachim in shared esteem for Liszt, but the friendship broke up when Joachim wrote a letter disavowing Liszt in 1857 and later, in 1860, signed the manifesto attacking the New German school. In 1866, Bülow undertook an initiative to restore their friendship (he had never ceased admiring Joachim's talent at interpreting Beethoven), but the relationship remained strained. In 1868 Joachim was called to become the director of the newly established college of music in Berlin, where he lived until his death in 1907.

8. As he mentioned in his reply to Bülow's congratulatory telegram (no. 11), Brahms had been invited by the Duke and Duchess of Meiningen to spend the second half of May at the ducal family's summer residence, the Villa Carlotta near Cadenabbia on Lake Como (cf. BBW XVII, p. 24) but hesitated to accept the invitation. He did not go there that year, but in September of the next year he did briefly visit the Villa Carlotta on a trip to Italy.

9. Franziska von Bülow (1800–1888), née Stoll, married as of 1828 to Eduard von Bülow (1803–1855); Bülow's parents were divorced in 1849.

10. Wüllner supervised the 59th Lower Rhine Music Festival in Aachen. Pianist and conductor Franz Wüllner (1832–1902) had been one of Brahms's friends since 1853. Important stages of his career were the office of the first court orchestra conductor in Munich in 1871 (as successor to Bülow, where he conducted the premières of *Rhinegold* and *The Valkyrie*); director of the Dresden Conservatory in 1877; and successor to Ferdinand Hiller the municipal orchestra conductor and director of the music conservatory at Cologne in 1884.

11. During his time in Dresden, Wüllner had shared the conducting of the Dresden court orchestra with Ernst von Schuch (1846–1914); in 1882 he was excluded from directing the opera in favor of Schuch.

Letter No. 13

Sign.: Mus. ep. Hans von Bülow 292. One double page, written on two sides (1r+2r), at the top left a printed half-profile portrait of Brahms.

1. Publius Vergilius Maro (70 to 90 CE), *Aeneis* 2:3: *Infandum, regina, iubes renovare dolorem.*

2. Emil Krause (1840–1916) lived in Hamburg as of 1860, teaching piano and music theory (as of 1885 he taught at the conservatory). The letter refers to Krause's pedagogic work, published in 1882 in six booklets under the title *Ein Beitrag zum Studium der Technik des Clavierspiels in 100 Übungen*, op. 38 (100 Exercises for the Study of Piano Technique, op. 38). Bülow had done Krause the favor of writing a short recommendation for it which the publisher (Johann August Böhme in Hamburg) then placed in the advertisement (cf. *Allgemeine Deutsche Musikzeitung* 9, no. 22 [9 June 1882]: p. 198). Bülow played on the title, writing, "Very modest, indeed. This contribution [to the study of piano technique] is so exhaustive and replete as to render other works of its kind entirely superfluous; it is a *compendium*, an enchiridion in the true sense of the word, the product of years of thought on theory and practice, a bright mind, and the heart of one who has devoted himself to teaching with self-sacrificing enthusiasm. The piano-playing world will welcome the work more than colleagues, who, though they may have produced valuable exercise books of their own, will probably see them humbled and even supplanted by this new work at the height of current development that with logical clarity makes use of all the innovations in piano technique. A glance through it shows that it recommends itself and needs no further praise. Hamburg, 20 March 1882, Hans von Bülow." Bülow's letter no. 13 is a reply to an undated letter from Brahms, whose attention had apparently been drawn to Krause's op. 38 by Bülow's text in the advertisement. Brahms wrote,

> *I have just read your lines about Krause's studies (Emil Krause). I would feel very pressed to order them immediately, if only you hadn't combined flattery with insult! So let me ask whether in the meantime you couldn't send me one or the other of the booklets by mail to let me have a look? I am curious to see whether someone else has already completed my own major life's task!* (BBS VII [6], p. 187, footnote 1)

At this time Brahms had already begun compiling his own work of etudes. It was, however, not published until 1893 and titled *51 Studies for the Piano*.

3. The ironic comment draws on the title of a collection of etudes called *L'indispensable du pianiste: Excercices quotidiens pour le Piano*, op. 100 (1851) by Antoine de Kontski (1817–1899). In "Travel Reviews" written in 1877, Bülow quoted Liszt's reply to de Kontski, who in Weimar in 1852 had personally given him a copy of the exercises:

> Dear Friend, if you feel like producing more humbug, then make it at least less rococo. You see, I , for my person, not being entirely inexperienced, know of only *one* thing that is really *indispensable du pianiste*, namely a good pair of trousers. (BBS III/2, p. 164)

Once, though, Bülow did use the expression *l'indispensable du pianiste* approvingly, namely, in referring to etudes by J. B. Cramer, which Bülow himself reedited (BBS III/1, p. 249).

4. The sample notes are quoted from the beginning of Felix Mendelssohn's Symphony no. 3, op. 56, called "The Scottish Symphony," here alluding to Brahms's frugality in asking Bülow to send him a free copy. As evidenced by the index of his musical possessions, Brahms did eventually buy Krause's book of exercises (Hofmann, p. 156).

5. Brahms's reply to Bülow's suggestion had been,

> *The fact that I cannot make up my mind about Bayreuth is probably a sign that a "yes" just refuses to surface. I hardly need tell you that the Wagnerians frighten me and that could spoil any pleasure I would get from the best Wagner. I don't have plans yet, and I might hide behind my beard that always lets me wander about so nicely anonymously.* (Taken from Kalbeck 3/1, p. 84, footnote)

In a letter to his wife, Bülow mentioned this reply from Brahms, which apparently was not the latter's last word on the topic (cf. letter no. 14, note no. 5): "Got news from Brahms in Ischl. He's not going to Bayreuth. I don't feel like it anymore either. As beautiful as the poetry is, the music for *Parsifal* is just too convulsive" (BBS VII [6], p. 188, footnote 1).

Later Bülow did revive his plan to see a *Parsifal* performance, however, and went to Bayreuth in the summer of 1884 (as we know from his daughter Daniela in Richard Wagner, *Briefe an Hans von Bülow*, edited by Daniela Thode [Jena, 1916], p. xxxvi).

6. The "false Demetrius arrangement" is the *Parsifal* piano arrangement devised by Josef Rubinstein (1847–1884); it is a "fake" Demetrius compared to the "real" one by the "real," namely, Anton Rubinstein (1829–1894). Demetrius was the son of Ivan the Terrible; after his murder by Boris Goduno in 1591, several pretenders to the throne used his name.

7. Cf. letter no. 12, note 10.

Letter No. 14

Sign.: Mus. ep. Hans von Bülow 293. One double page, written on two sides (1r+2r) plus one postscript written on 1v (lengthwise).

1. Bülow was right in assuming that it was Brahms who had Simrock send him a preprint copy of the score for Piano Concerto no. 2. Taking up Bülow's comment from the third-to-last paragraph of letter no. 13, Brahms had written on 8 July 1882 to Simrock, "*Now Bülow is sitting alone in Meiningen studying it, and wouldn't it seem friendly, if he were to get the very first copy?!*" (BBW X, p. 215). This copy was not found among Bülow's remaining papers. His estate did, however, include the main part for the arrangement for two pianos (Simrock; pub. no. 8260) with a few fingering marks made by Bülow (SBB, Sign.: Kb 541; together with op. 15).

2. Franz Liszt.

3. Richard Wagner.

4. In the *Bayreuther Blättern* (Bayreuth Pages) in July 1882 Richard Wagner had published remarks titled an "Open Letter to Mr. Friedrich Schön in Worms" expressing the ironic speculation that in the future the same thing would happen with Beethoven's music as happened for the "posterity of the barbarian immigration, for whom only a few of Sophocles' and Aeschylus' works survived, compared to most of Euripides' tragedies; so, too, then, will about nine Brahms symphonies survive for our descendants, but at most two of Beethoven's; because plagiarists close ranks with progress." *Complete Works and Poetry*, vol. 10, 6th ed. (Leipzig, no date), p. 293.

5. Brahms refers to this prophecy of Wagner's in a letter of regret returning to Bülow an entrance ticket that Bülow had sent him for Bayreuth:

> *As it happens, I've promised to be in Ischl from the 4th to the 6th* [of August] *for a visit. How unfortunate, since for the rest of the month I have no other plans than to make a pilgrimage to the oracle that makes such kind predictions.* (Taken from Kalbeck 3/2, p. 346)

That, despite the dismissal of the plan noted in letter no. 13, the idea of a trip to Bayreuth—which incidentally never did happen—had not yet been entirely abandoned by Brahms can be seen in his correspondence with Simrock, to whom he wrote on 30 July 1882,

> *Now, if you should happen to journey to Bayreuth, I would very gladly accompany you! And if you'd like me to, I believe it would be good to decide as soon as possible. After the 6th I am available for any date. . . . Twice I've been offered a free ticket but was unable to go! It looks like I'm going to have to spend 30 marks for it.* (BBW X, p. 218f; cf. also p. 220)

6. Six Songs for Voice and Piano, op. 85, and Six Songs for Low Voice and Piano, op. 86, apparently sent to Bülow by Brahms (both printed in July

Brahms's Piano Concerto No. 2 with fingering by Bülow (cf. letter no. 14, note 1). *Staatsbibliothek zu Berlin—Preussischer Kulturbesitz; SBB Kb 541*

1882, referred to in Bülow's letter no. 12 and in Brahms's previous letter to that one).

7. Alludes to Robert Franz (1815–1892), whose printed oeuvre consists mainly of songs very widespread in the nineteenth century.

8. Robert Schumann.

9. Ferdinand David (1810–1873), as of 1835 concertmaster for the Leipzig Gewandhaus Orchestra and after 1843 violin teacher at the conservatory. On 18 March 1845 he played the solo part of Mendelssohn's Violin Concerto op. 64 at its premier performance.

10. According to Richard Strauss, Bülow's "small hand could barely reach an octave." Richard Strauss, *Betrachtungen und Erinnerungen*, ed. Willi Schuh (Munich, 1989), p. 207 [*Recollections and Reflections* (London, 1953)].

11. Doris Raff, née Genast (1826–1912), widow of composer Joachim Raff who died on 25 June 1882 in Frankfurt/Main (cf. letter no. 17, note 2).

Letter No. 15

Sign.: Mus. ep. Hans von Bülow 294. One double page, written on three sides (1r+v, 2r).

1. Princess Marie Elisabeth (1853–1923), the sole daughter of George II. She had taken piano lessons from, among others, Theodor Kirchner (1872/73). (On Kirchner see letter no. 49, note 4.)

2. In a letter to his daughter Daniela (dated 12 October 1883; *New Letters*, p. 597) Bülow said that Meiningen is "actually only a freight train station."

Letter No. 16

Sign.: Mus. ep. Hans von Bülow 295. One double page, written on two sides (1r+2r) printed letterhead as in ep. no. 284.

1. Cf. letter no. 10, note 2. Notes 1, 2, and 3 refer to enclosed texts (that did not survive with the letter), probably reviews of the performance of Johannes Brahms's Symphony no. 3, op. 90 (performed on 2 December 1883 in Vienna).

2. Eduard Hanslick (1825–1904), a music critic (as of 1864 for Vienna's *Neue Freie Presse*) and (as of 1870) professor for the history of music at the Vienna University, was one of the most influential pioneers for Brahms in Vienna. As of 1862 they were friends.

3. Ludwig Speidel (1830–1906), theater critic for the *Neue Freie Presse* and music critic for Vienna's *Fremdenblatt*. His antagonistic attitude toward Brahms always vexed Bülow. [Bülow plays with the name, based on the phrase *Galle speien*—to spew gall. CK]

4. Henriette Fritsch-Estrangin, mentioned until the late 1870s as Henriette Fritsch in correspondence between Brahms and Clara Schumann as being a piano pupil of Clara Schumann's. After marrying she lived in Marseille. She had been to the premier performance of Brahms's Symphony no. 3 on 2 December 1883, and afterward joined Brahms's circle of friends to celebrate.

5. There is no evidence that Brahms ever wrote the duke a letter of introduction for Henriette Fritsch-Estrangin.

6. Sophie Menter (1846–1918), took piano lessons with Lebert, Tausig, and Liszt. Her younger sister Eugenie (born in 1853) took lessons with Bülow when he taught at the royal school of music in Munich.

7. Hermann Levi (1839–1900) was court orchestra conductor in Munich from 1872 to 1896, when he retired. As such, he conducted the subscription concerts at Munich's Music Academy. Brahms and Levi were friends as of the mid-1860s. An estrangement grew between them when in the course of the 1870s Levi began to make his mark as an interpreter of Wagner.

8. Max Kalbeck.

9. Ludwig Speidel.

10. Allusion to Johann Herbeck (1831–1877), conductor of the Vienna Society of the Friends of Music and for a time (1870–1875) director at the Vienna Court Opera. After resigning from directing the opera, Herbeck once again took up conducting concerts for the Society of the Friends of Music, a position that Brahms vacated for him. Brahms's friends, however, thought that Herbeck "had pushed him out." George Fischer, ed., *Letters from Theodor Billroth* (Hanover & Leipzig [2], 1896), p. 191.

11. Cf. letter no. 14, note 4.

Letter No. 17

Sign.: Mus. ep. Hans von Bülow 296. One double page, written on two sides (1r+2r).

1. Bülow means the first Brahms concert that the Meiningen court orchestra gave in Berlin (on 8 January 1882 in the auditorium of the *Singakademie*) after which Brahms offered Bülow the privilege of addressing him with the German personal form *Du*, instead of the formal address *Sie*. [It implies a more intimate friendship, and the mutual decision is usually sealed with a kiss. Cf. letter no. 10. CK] January 8 is Bülow's birthday.

2. Composer Joachim Raff (1822–1882), befriended with Bülow since the latter's days at secondary school in Stuttgart (1846–1848). From 1849 to 1853 Raff was Liszt's assistant and secretary in Weimar. He settled in

Wiesbaden as a piano teacher, and from 1877 until his death he was the director of the newly established Hoch Conservatory in Frankfurt/Main.

3. This "act of propaganda" for one of Joachim Raff's works occurred not, as Bülow mistakenly recalls, on Bülow's birthday (8 Jan. 1848), but on the evening of New Year's Day: Item number five on the program of a mixed concert in Stuttgart's imperial palace Redoute Hall for 1 January 1848 was a performance by the schoolboy Hans von Bülow (his first proven public appearance), playing a "Piano Fantasy on a theme from Küken's [*sic*] *Pretenders* by J. Raff." (The printed program is among Bülow's remaining papers; SBB, Sign.: Db 1815 [1]). The work itself has been lost.

Letter No. 18

Sign.: Mus. ep. Hans von Bülow 297. One double page, written on three sides (1r+v, 2r).

1. A German saying: "The people of Nuremberg don't even hang the ones they catch." Cf. Karl Simrock, ed., *Die deutschen Sprichwörter* [German Sayings] (Frankfurt/Main, 1846), p. 209.

2. Cf. letter no. 1, note 3, for Bülow's way of counting Brahms's symphonies as the next numbers of Beethoven's.

Conducted by Bülow, the Meiningen court orchestra played Brahms's Symphony no. 2, op. 73, on 10 January 1884 in Würzburg. They played Brahms's Symphony no. 1 the next day, 11 January 1884, in Nuremberg.

3. *Verweile doch, Du bist so schön.* Johann Wolfgang von Goethe (1749–1832), *Faust: Der Tragödie erster Teil*, verse 1700.

4. Organist Johann Georg Herzog (1822–1909) had been director of music at the university in Erlangen since 1854.

5. Beethoven: Overture to "Leonore" no. 3, op. 72.

The program for the Meiningen court orchestra's concert in Erlangen on 13 January 1884 read, Weber: "Oberon" Overture; Beethoven: Symphony no. 8, op. 93; Beethoven: Piano Concerto no. 5, op. 73 (solo by Bülow; conducted by Mannstädt); Beethoven: Symphony no. 5, op. 67; Brahms: Academic Festival Overture op. 80.

6. The program for the Meiningen court orchestra's concert in Frankfurt on 21 January 1884 read, Berlioz: King Lear Overture; Brahms: Symphony no. 1, op. 68; Beethoven: Third movement (Adagio) from Symphony no. 9, op. 125; Brahms: Haydn Variations op. 56a; Weber: Overtures from "Freischütz," "Euryanthe," and "Oberon."

7. Clara Schumann (1819–1896), teacher for piano as of 1878 at the Hoch Conservatory in Frankfurt. She scheduled a concert of her pupils at the conservatory for 1 January 1884—the same day the Meiningen court orchestra

performed a purely Beethoven concert in the evening. She did, however, attend the Meiningen court orchestra's concert on 21 January. Her diary page for 21 January 1884 mentions Bülow:

> He rehearses the same way he plays, plucking everything apart and dissecting it—nothing's left for the heart to do. It's all headwork, calculation.

Berthold Litzmann, *Clara Schumann: Ein Künstlerleben* [Life of an Artist], vol. 3 (Leipzig [2], 1909), p. 448.

8. Beethoven.

9. A play on Robert Fuchs (1847–1927), professor at the Vienna Conservatory as of 1875, known predominately for his orchestra serenades op. 9, 14, 21, 51, and 53.

10. Hermann Graedener (1844–1929), son of Hamburg's conductor and composer Carl G. P. Graedener (1812–1883). Brahms and Bülow were well acquainted with the latter. Hermann Graedener, who lived in Vienna since his days as a student at the Vienna Conservatory, became an instructor for music theory at the Vienna Conservatory in 1877. Bülow's letter alludes to his Orchestra Capriccio op. 4.

11. Franz Liszt, who, without settling anywhere permanently during the last decades of his life, lived periodically in Rome, Weimar, and (Buda-)Pest, had composed in 1883 a "Bülow March" for the piano that he published (at Schlesinger in Berlin) early in 1884 with the following dedication:

> For thirty years Hans von Bülow has meant, labored at and promoted noble, accurate, high-minded, and liberal performances in the world of music. As a virtuoso, docent, conductor, commentator and propagandist, at times even as a humorous journalist, Bülow, with his god-given innate motivation and passionate perseverance, his unyielding heroic pursuit of the ideal, achieving it when possible, remains the *umpire* of musical progress. New proof of which can be witnessed in his conducting of the Meiningen Court Orchestra, to whom the undersigned dedicates this Bülow March out of esteem for its exemplary symphonic performance. /*F. Liszt*/ January 84, Weimar.

12. Eduard Hanslick.

13. Brahms replied with a letter discovered just a few years ago:

[Vienna, 14 January 1884]
Dear Friend,
In two hours I'll be departing for Wiesbaden, but first I want to finally send you a brief, most heartfelt word of thanks for the many amusing, delightful greetings you have sent me. Day after day I intend to write with devotion. But that's the problem!

With all the pressing and annoying correspondence I must complete every day, I just can't get it done, and prefer to get such beautiful large stationery from others like you than to fill it myself.

On the 21st I will probably have to entertain a bit in Wiesbaden. But I plan nonetheless around the 29th to come and ruin your vacation. I look forward to spending a few wonderful mornings with you and your superb orchestra. I hope your wife will be in town, and not on vacation, so that in the morning I'll look forward to the evening! That will put me in the right mood to proceed to Leipzig with a dab of Bülow, as much as possible.

Now continue your triumphal tour, your present way of giving concerts is ideal!

Best greetings to you and yours!

Cordially subservient,

J. Brahms

The original German letter was published by Styra Avins in "The 'Excellent People' of the Meiningen Court Orchestra and the Third Symphony of Johannes Brahms," in *Spätphase(n)? Johannes Brahms' Werke der 1880er und 1890er Jahre*, ed. Maren Goltz, Wolfgang Sandberger, and Christiane Wiesenfeldt (Munich, 2008), p. 33.

Postcard, No. 19

Sign.: Mus. ep. Hans von Bülow 298. Preprinted postcard issued by the Deutsche Reichspost; stamped in Meiningen on 28 May 1884 / arrived in Dusseldorf on 29 May 1884.

1. Dusseldorf, where Brahms conducted his Symphony no. 3, op. 90, on 2 June 1884 at the 61st Lower Rhine Music Festival.

Letter No. 20

Sign.: Mus. ep. Hans von Bülow 299. One double page, written on three sides (1r+v, 2r).

1. In June 1884 Bülow for the first time taught summer courses for piano at the Frankfurt Raff Conservatory (further courses followed in 1885, 1886, and 1887). Following Joachim Raff's death in 1882, part of the Hoch Conservatory split off in April 1883 out of protest against the newly designated director's (Bernhard Scholz) personnel policy; Bülow took on the honorary presidency for the new conservatory (cf. also letter no. 45, note 9). Bülow donated his income from this work to a committee for erecting a monument to Raff, of which he was a founding member.

2. *Schmalarsch*, *Weichel*, and *Mostrich*: Small butt, softie, and mustard stand for Breitkopf & Härtel (broad head and Hard's son) and Senff (mustard).

Brahms's publishers profited from Bülow's summer courses because pupils purchased sheet music. "Breitkopf & Härtel" and "Bartholf Senff" were Brahms's publishers in Leipzig. The groaner "small butt & softie" was first used by Richard Wagner; cf. Wagner's letter to Bülow dated 3 February 1854. Richard Wagner, *Complete Letters*, vol. 6, p. 77f., n. 15.

Brahms's works for piano published at Breitkopf & Härtel (before Simrock acquired the rights in 1888) are Sonatas op. 1 and op. 2, Scherzo op. 4, Schumann Variations op. 9, Ballades op. 10, and the Handel Variations op. 24. Senff had published Sonata op. 5, etudes for the piano, and the Gluck arrangement (Gavotte).

3. Bernhard Scholz (1835–1916) followed Joachim Raff as director of the Hoch Conservatory in 1883. Scholz had been one of the four (along with Brahms, Joachim, and Grimm) that in 1860 had signed the manifesto against the New German school of music.

4. After Bülow's concert agent Hermann Wolff (cf. letter no. 22, note 6) refused to shoulder the financial risk for the Austrian segment of the Meiningen orchestra's tour through the south, the Vienna publisher Albert Gutmann (later known as Anton Bruckner's publisher) deposited the guarantee sum. Bülow calls Gutmann the "nonpublisher" (Non-Simrock) of Symphony no. 3 because after its premier performance in Vienna on 2 December 1883, Gutmann publicly (as was not customary) announced in Vienna that he would offer 10,000 marks for it. Brahms, however, was not impressed.

5. The tour's final schedule was Oct. 31, Würzburg; Nov. 1, Mannheim; Nov. 2, Neustadt a.d.H.; Nov. 3 and 4, Frankfurt; Nov. 5, Karlsruhe; Nov. 6, Wiesbaden; Nov. 7 and 8, Strasbourg; Nov. 9 and 10, Freiburg; Nov. 11, Karlsruhe; Nov. 12, 13, and 14, Stuttgart; Nov. 15, Munich; Nov. 16, Augsburg; Nov. 17 and 18, Munich; Nov. 20, Vienna; Nov. 21, Pressburg; Nov. 22 and 24, (Buda-)Pest; Nov. 25, Vienna; Nov. 26 and 28, Graz; Nov. 30, Brno; Dec. 2, Vienna (later an additional concert was added for Vienna on Dec. 1); Dec. 3 and 4, Prague; and Dec. 5, Dresden. Immediately following all of this, the Meiningen season opened with its first subscription concert on 7 December 1884.

6. Mrs. Von Heldburg (cf. letter no. 6, note 1).

7. On Villa Carlotta, see letter no. 12, note 8.

8. Brahms's Symphony no. 3.

9. The title of Léo Delibes's (1836–1891) last opera, performed for the first time on 14 April 1883 in Paris, is *Lakmé*.

[Bülow's intention is to shock the audience in Bayreuth by comparing endeavors there with the shallow, but enormously successful Parisian opera *Lakmé*. On 2 July 1883 Bülow had written to his wife Marie: "Delibes's *Lakmé* is a great disappointment. He should have stuck to composing ballet, like Joh.

Strauss stuck with waltzes and polkas. Affected, stale jargon, though not lacking taste, not vulgar . . . . by comparison, Bizet's *Carmen* is the purest Mozart."
(I thank Frithjof Haas for this explanation.) CK]

10. After Wagner's death some circles in Bayreuth had suggested to
Bülow that he should rejoin the Wagner community. Cf. Ludwig Schemann,
Hans von Bülow im Lichte der Wahrheit (Regensburg, 1935), pp. 50–52. Cosima
Wagner, too, planned to ask Bülow to direct all the musical dramas, starting
in 1885, for which Wagner had not already made arrangements that they be
directed by others (the *Ring* was to be directed by Hans Richter, and *Parsifal*
by Hermann Levi). Cf. Dietrich Mack, ed., *Cosima Wagner: Das zweite Leben;
Briefe und Aufzeichnungen, 1883–1930* (Munich, 1980), p. 35.

On Bülow's attending a *Parsifal* performance shortly after writing this
letter, see letter no. 13, note 5.

Letter No. 21

*Sign.: Mus. ep. Hans von Bülow 300. One double page, written on three sides
(1r, 2r, 1v [lengthwise]), black mourning border.*

1. Regarding the date, Marie von Bülow's edition dates this letter as being from "between October 10 and 14." Bülow more likely wrote it at the
same time he replied to Gutmann on 9 October (see note 4 below), respond-
ing to the latter's letter that arrived simultaneously with the Brahms letter
mentioned (see note 2 below).

2. Albert Gutmann (cf. letter no. 20, note 4). Brahms had written,

> *Gutmann was here, enormously giddy with excitement, as if your concerts had been*
> Parsifal *performances. He has all sorts of ideas and if an overture is the first thing on
> the program, he can think of a hundred others that could be first just as well.* (BBS
> VII [6], p. 301, footnote 1)

3. Vienna's executioner.

4. At the same time, Bülow wrote on 9 October 1884 to Gutmann
suggesting the order of pieces for the second concert in Vienna (the first of
two Brahms evenings), saying that only this "well-considered" order of the
three symphonies contains a "climax" (BBS VII [6], p. 303). Bülow's correspondence with Gutmann (dated 18 Oct. 1884) also reveals how long, under
Bülow's interpretation, each of the three symphonies lasts: "I lasts 37 minutes,
II lasts 38, III takes 34 minutes. (However, in I and II we skip the [exposi-
tion] repeat of the first movement, which the Master has authorized me to
do!)" (BBS VII [6], p. 305). Gutmann refused Bülow's program suggestion,
and thus the final programs of the last two concerts in Vienna were not purely
Brahms evenings. From Brahms they only included, on 25 November, Piano
Concerto no. 1, op. 15 (solo by Bülow), and Symphony no. 3, op. 90, and

on 2 December, Piano Concerto no. 2, op. 83 (solo by Brahms), and Haydn Variations op. 56a.

5. Joachim Raff's overtures for Shakespeare's dramas *Romeo and Juliet* and *Macbeth* were published as No. 1 and No. 2 of "four Shakespeare overtures for a large orchestra" in 1891 (at Schmidt in Boston and Leipzig). No. 3 and No. 4 were never published.

6. Bülow toured Russia and the Baltic provinces in January 1885, conducting Brahms's Symphony no. 3, op. 90 (on Jan. 10), and playing Piano Concerto no. 2 (on Jan. 24) in Petersburg. He also played piano works by Brahms (Sonata op. 5, Scherzo op. 4, and the Intermezzo and Capriccio from op. 76) in Petersburg, Moscow, Warsaw, Helsinki, Dorpat, and Riga.

7. Bülow's appearance in Munich as "Levi *al rovescio*" had several facets. First of all, as of 1872, Hermann Levi (cf. letter no. 16, note 7) conducted the royal orchestra (in other words, he held the position previously held by Bülow). Second, Levi started as a disciple of Brahms but then became a Wagnerian, eventually even directing a Wagner premier performance (*Parsifal* in 1882)—in other words, his career took the opposite direction of Bülow's. Third, Bülow and his concert agent Hermann Wolff allowed themselves the practical joke of announcing the Meiningen orchestra's three guest performances in Munich as "subscription concerts"—as if they were playing at home (1: 15 Nov. 1884 [Beethoven], 2: 17 Nov. 1884 [Brahms], and 3: 18 Nov. 1884 [Berlioz, Schubert, Raff, Weber]; an additional matinee was given on 18 Nov. 1884 [Rheinberger, R. Strauss, and Raff]). Following the Brahms concert, Bülow wrote to his wife, alluding to Levi, "Now Brahms has definitely been enthroned here. One day of mine [with my Meiningen orchestra] accomplished *more* than a Levitical decade" (BBS VII [6], p. 318).

8. Marcus Tullius Cicero (106–43 BC), *Ad Quintum Fratrem* 2,8: "in hac causa mihi aqua haeret." Bülow's principle of having the various sections of the orchestra practice separately is said to be what interested Brahms in working with Bülow and the Meiningen orchestra in the first place (Kalbeck 3/2, p. 306).

Letter No. 22

Sign.: Mus. ep. Hans von Bülow 301. One double page, written on three sides (1e, 2r, 1v [lengthwise]).

1. In a letter written from Mürzzuschlag in mid-October 1884 Brahms replied to Bülow's request to ask Simrock about publishing Raff's overtures as follows:

Dear Friend,
*   I am returning to Vienna tomorrow, but before I leave and while I'm packing I would like to write you a few words—if only I knew what to write!*

It is not Simrock's custom at all to do things like what you are requesting. I, for instance, paid cash myself to have Marxsen's 100 variations printed. What you want is just as understandable as it is difficult!

To my knowledge, Simrock has never published anything by Raff; it is idle to ask whether he ever wanted or wants to. We both can imagine what he would casually say about it. And it would be impossible for him to accept the works as a gift.

I am trying to think of a solution, but what concerns me more is—the composer himself!

I tend to deeply envy my prolific colleagues who compose with such ease and speed. I assume that they don't write music simply to be mentioned one day in an encyclopedia, but because they feel the same need, have the same reasons that I do—namely, the best ones. How often does one of them happily write a fine that really means "I'm finished saying what I wanted to say!"? How long I myself carry the tiniest completed composition around with me, before reluctantly admitting that it's done!

But Raff composes four overtures in passing for four of the greatest tragedies. How enviable, to be able to satisfy oneself so easily and so often and feel so liberated. Did Raff take time for hangovers? He was smart enough! Or was he simply glad to have talent?

The lesser of us are rarely guilty of that. Yet look how much we lesser talents can achieve!

Now, regarding Simrock, what should I do? Are you really proud of these pieces? Are you going to enthusiastically perform them? What do Raff's usual publishers say about them?

We can continue this discussion when we meet, but let me just add now that I will not be traveling to Russia or England because my appetite for concerts finds more than enough fodder on meadows around here.

> *Forgive this confused letter, I've been packing all the while!*
> *Sincerely,*
> *Your Joh. Brahms*

(Published in part in BBS VII [6], p. 307f; cited here from the original kept in the National Museum at Meiningen.)

The publication mentioned in the first paragraph is that of *100 Variations by Eduard Marxsen* that Brahms had printed at his own cost in 1883 for an anniversary of his teacher.

2. As Brahms mentions doing in the introductory and closing passages of his letter (see note 1 above).

3. Composer and violinist Sigismund Bachrich (1841–1913), composer and piano instructor Ignaz Brüll (1846–1907), and composer Anton Bruckner (1824–1896), here probably grouped together as "local colleagues" solely for the purpose of alliteration.

4. See note 4 to letter no. 20. Bülow had offered Gutmann to do an extra concert (in Vienna on 1 Dec. 1884) at the end of the Meiningen orchestra's

tour in Austria to cover any deficits the tour may have caused: "Piano Performance / Dr. Hans v. Bülow / In Cooperation with the Court Orchestra of His Highness the Duke of Saxe-Meiningen."

5. Bülow means that the Meiningen orchestra had fewer string players compared to the famous Vienna Philharmonic Orchestra that felt slighted by the Meiningen orchestra's appearances in Vienna. During this tour the orchestra from Meiningen had ten first and eight second violins, six violas, four cellos, and five basses—and then only when the pieces did not demand unusual instruments. For instance, when performing Wagner's A Faust Overture, the number of string players was diminished because some of them had to play the piccolo flute, third bassoon, tenor trombone, bass trombone, and tuba (cf. BBS VII [6], p. 304).

Contrary to Bülow's suggestion, none of the three programs in Vienna (20 Nov., 25 Nov., 2 Dec.) contained the Academic Festival Overture. The second concert on 25 November 1884 closed with Beethoven's Leonore Overture no. 3.

6. Concert agent Hermann Wolff (1845–1905) had been in contact with Bülow since 1880 (working before then for Anton Rubinstein). As of 1882 he organized the Meiningen orchestra's concert tours, making a name for himself as a concert agent. Later he also organized Bülow's subscription concerts in Hamburg and concerts for the Philharmonic Orchestra in Berlin.

7. Literally, Bülow writes that Wolff "will ask you to *chlorify* [disinfect] one of our *plague* concerts," making a pun out of the German meaning for *Pest*, which is "plague."

In the second of the two concerts that the Meiningen orchestra subsequently gave in Budapest (the first on 22 Nov., the second on 24 Nov.), Brahms did play the solo part in his Piano Concerto no. 2.

8. Fritz Steinbach (1855–1916). From 1880 to 1886, Steinbach was the second orchestra conductor in Mainz; from 1886 to 1902 he succeeded Bülow as conductor in Meiningen.

9. Cf. letter no. 16, note 7, and letter no. 21, note 7.

10. Hans Richter (1843–1916) was a trained horn player and had conducted the orchestra in Munich in 1868–1869 under Bülow's supervision. In Vienna, at the height of his career, Richter was conductor of the royal orchestra, director of the philharmonic concerts, and concert director for the Society of the Friends of Music. From the start, in 1876, Richter had been one of the main conductors at the Bayreuth festivals.

11. Felix Mottl (1856–1911) conducted the royal orchestra in Karlsruhe as of 1881. Bülow's esteem for Mottl was longstanding; when, in 1886, Mottl was chosen to conduct *Tristan and Isolde* at the Bayreuth Festival, Bülow expressed his explicit approval in a letter to his daughter Daniela (dated 8 June 1886; *New Letters*, p. 635).

12. [It is unclear what Bülow meant by the echoism *Wenden-Base*; it was perhaps a running joke.]

No. 23—Postcard

Sign.: Mus. ep. Hans von Bülow 302. Preprinted postcard form from the German Reichspost; stamped in Meiningen on 31 March 1885 and in Wieden, Vienna, on 2 April 1885.

1. Pleissenland is an area located on the River Pleisse in what is now Thuringia and Saxony.

The notes shown begin the finale of Symphony no. 3, op. 90, that the audience at a concert in Leipzig on 29 March 1885 demanded that the orchestra repeat. [Bülow makes a pun on *capieren* (to grasp, figuratively) and *da capo*, inventing a neoverb *dacapieren* (to repeat); translated here loosely as "they *got it* so well that we *gave it* to them again." CK]

The program that night in Leipzig had included Berlioz's "Corsair" Overture; Brahms's Symphony no. 3, op. 90; Wagner's A Faust Overture; and Beethoven's Symphony no. 9, op. 125, movements 1 through 3.

2. Hans Richter (cf. letter no. 22, note 10) had conducted the premier performance of Symphony no. 3 in Vienna on 2 December 1882.

Letter No. 24

Sign. Mus. ep. Hans von Bülow 303. One double page, written on three sides (1r, 2r, 1v [lengthwise]).

1. In return for a birthday present that Bülow had sent him (see note 2 below), Brahms sent Bülow a pencil copy Beethoven had made of a piece by Palestrina. It was not found among Bülow's remaining papers. In the accompanying letter, Brahms wrote,

> *Most kind of all Friends,*
> *Thank you so much for remembering my birthday on the 7th of May. The joy at seeing your handwriting normally increases with the number of pages! But this time—and with such an enclosure—you could have spared words! Since I have unintentionally become somewhat of a collector, you found the perfect gift. Until now I didn't have one page by Berlioz. And to see this Ophelia dated the 7th of May particularly touches me; no one is guarded against such very tender sentiment.*
> *But my classical enclosure does well repay you for the unholy and the Frenchman, doesn't it? Beethoven copies a hymn by Palestrina! Well then, thank you so much, I believe you will read it in Meiningen where you are enjoying some comfortable rest.* (BBS VII [6], p. 364)

2. For his fifty-second birthday, Bülow had sent Brahms a handwritten piece by Berlioz that Berlioz himself had dated 7 May 1842 (Brahms's birthday). In his index of musical belongings Brahms noted the fact specifically: "*Berlioz*, Hector, handwriting: *La mort d'Ophelie* (ballade with pianoforte), 7 May 1842" (Hofmann, p. 149).

3. Friedrich Schiller (1759–1805). The phrase is taken from Schiller's *Xenien*: "When kings build, the wagoners have work" ("Kant and His Interpreters").

4. On Bülow's summer courses at the Raff Conservatory, see letter no. 20, note 1.

5. Franz Mannstädt (1852–1932) began to assist Bülow at conducting in Meiningen on 1 September 1882, at first temporarily, but after March 1884 permanently, in order to have an income that would allow him to tour as a concert pianist. George II, however, did not consent to Bülow's request to hand over management of the orchestra's business details to Mannstädt. In the spring of 1885 Mannstädt left Meiningen to become conductor of the philharmonic orchestra in Berlin, which he was until 1887, and then once again from 1893 to 1897.

6. Richard Strauss (1864–1949). Bülow organized that in June 1885 Richard Strauss was employed to replace Mannstädt as assistant conductor in Meiningen. (Other applicants for the position were Gustav Mahler (1860–1911), Jean Louis Nicodé (1853–1919), Felix Weingartner (1863–1942), and Herman Zumpe (1850–1903).

Letter no. 25

Sign.: Mus. ep. Hans von Bülow 304. One double page, written on two sides (1r, 2r).

1. Brahms had announced his visit and—in his typical manner—mentioned having just completed Symphony no. 4:

Dear, esteemed Friend,

Unfortunately nothing became of the piano concerto that I would have liked to have written. I don't know whether the first two are too good or too bad, but they are an obstacle.

But a few Entr'acts are lying around, together making what I guess you'd normally call a symphony. On the road during concert tours with the Meiningen orchestra I often imagined nice and comfortably trying it out with all of you, and I still do, but I wonder whether it will attract any more audience! I'm afraid it smacks of the climate here—the cherries are sour, you wouldn't eat them! Unfortunately I only know one skilled copier here in Vienna and he will not return (with Strauss's orchestra) until September 15. (Quoted from Kalbeck 3/2, p. 447)

2. Gaius Plinius Secundus sen. (AD 23/24–79). *Historia naturalis*: "Nulla dies sine linea!" Bülow's alteration of the phrase to characterize the Meiningen orchestra's fall tour ("Not a day without a concert!") is entirely correct. The final schedule was as follows: Frankfurt, Nov. 3; Siegen, Nov. 4; Dortmund, Nov. 5; Essen, Nov. 6; Elberfeld, Nov. 7 and 8; Düsseldorf, Nov. 9; Rotterdam, Nov. 10; Utrecht, Nov. 11; Amsterdam, Nov. 12 and 13; The Hague, Nov. 14; Haarlem, Nov. 15; Arnheim, Nov. 16; Utrecht, Nov. 17; The Hague, Nov. 18; Rotterdam, Nov. 19; Amsterdam, Nov. 20; Krefeld, Nov. 21; Bonn, Nov. 22; Cologne, Nov. 23; Frankfurt, Nov. 24. (Followed by a purely Brahms concert in Wiesbaden on November 25, directed by the composer himself.)

Brahms directed Symphony no. 4, op. 98, on 3, 6, 8, 11, 13, 14, 21, and 23 November. Bülow directed it on 19 November. Bülow had also originally planned to direct it at the final concert of the scheduled tour on 24 November, but a misunderstanding between Bülow and Brahms prevented him from doing so (see letter no. 26, note 5).

Letter No. 26

Sign.: Mus. ep. Hans von Bülow 306. One double page, written on three sides (1r+v, 2r).

Letter No. 27

Sign.: Mus. ep. Hans von Bülow 305. 1 double page, written on two sides (1r, 2r), printed letterhead: "Superintendent of the Ducal Court Orchestra Meiningen" and "Meiningen, —, 188-" (crossed out by Bülow).

1. Date taken from Marie von Bülow's edition of Bülow's letters (BBS VII [6], p. 381).

2. Richard Strauss succeeded Mannstädt as assistant conductor, giving his debut on 18 October 1885 at the second subscription concert playing Mozart's Piano Concerto in C minor KV 491 and directing his own Symphony in F minor op. 12. The program opened with Beethoven's Coriolan Overture and closed with Beethoven's Symphony no. 7, op. 92, both directed by Bülow.

3. Adolf Brodsky (1851–1929) played the violin solo in Brahms's Violin Concerto op. 77 on 25 October 1885. The second half of the program contained the premier performance of Brahms's Symphony no. 4, op. 98. Both works were directed by Brahms.

4. Cf. letter no. 8, note 1.

5. August Truckenbrodt (1840–1899) originally played the clarinet in the old Meiningen military music corps; as of 1869 he played the bassoon in the Meiningen court orchestra.

6. The symphony was heard for the first time (directed by Brahms) on 25 October 1885 at the third subscription concert. At the end of the performance, the duke requested that the first and third movements be repeated. The entire symphony was repeated on 1 November 1885 at the fourth subscription concert, directed by Bülow.

7. Alexander Friedrich, Landgrave of Hesse (1863–1945). Blind from birth, he had acquired profound training in music and was also a composer.

8. "Mozart's Adagio" was Brahms's nickname for Baroness von Heldburg. In response to letter no. 26 (with news of her serious illness), Brahms had written to Bülow:

> *It will be like hearing a Mozart symphony without the beautiful, noble adagio!*
> (BBS VII [6], p. 382, footnote 1)

By "replacement from Marseille" Bülow meant Henriette Fritsch-Estrangin (cf. letter no. 16, note 4).

Letter No. 28

Sign.: Mus. ep. Hans von Bülow 307. One double page, written on four sides (1r+v, 2r+v).

1. Cf. letter no. 27, note 5.

2. Cf. letter no. 27, note 3.

3. Bülow refers here to Brahms's suggestion, not only to put Symphony no. 4 at the orchestra's disposal, but to join the orchestra on tour:

> *my new symphony might be just the right thing for the Rhine and Dutch cities, where they always enjoy hearing my other works, and it would be fun to travel around a bit, either as a spare conductor or spare audience!* (Quoted from Geiringer, p. 172)

4. Cf. letter no. 15, note 1.

5. The tour began in Frankfurt on 3 November and was to end there on 24 November. On 3 November Brahms himself conducted his Symphony no. 4. The original plan was that Bülow would conduct it on 24 November (cf. letter no. 25, note 2). But things happened differently because of a letter that Brahms, during the tour, wrote to Bülow from Krefeld, to where Brahms had traveled ahead of the orchestra in order to celebrate the birthday of his friend Rudolf von der Leyen. On 17 November 1885 Brahms wrote,

> *Dearest Friend,*
> *my kind host Rudolf v. d. Leyen, insists that you stay with him instead of at the hotel. If you were going to spend days of leisure in Krefeld, I would advise you to*

take up his offer. But I have told him the opposite, namely, that for those few hours you would probably rather go to the hotel. And now I don't know what to tell you!

The trains leave Amsterdam at 7:15 and 10:20 and arrive here at 1:16 and 3:28 o'clock. If you arrive on the first one and leave on the last one on Sunday, then I insist that you come and stay with us! Otherwise, well, ponder it long or make a quick decision. Maybe you could just send a telegram: Leyen Co. Krefeld. Coming 1 1/4 [days], *or*: Leyen Co. Krefeld. Hotel please.

When I arrived here there were telegrams and letters from Frankfurt waiting for me, asking for the E minor for the museum, if you don't plan on using it in your second concert. I didn't bother you with the matter because I can make amends for my own foolishness. The people at Frankfurt have been so good to me that I'm angry at myself for having been so rude and inconsiderate!

But J. Br. is synonymous with awkwardness and such.

Cordial greetings. Everyone here is happy, particularly about your visit.

Cited from Kalbeck 3/2, p. 501f. For more context and the consequences this letter had, see the introduction to this volume.

Letter No. 29

Sign.: Mus. ep. Hans von Bülow 308. One double page, written on three sides (1r, 2r, 1v [lengthwise].

1. On 8 May 1886 Brahms had written to Bülow,

Dearest [Friend],

I've been told by Her Highness Princess Marie that you did not get the letter I wrote you right after our break-up this winter. It was a long, very serious, and well-meaning letter that I hoped would remedy the misunderstanding that troubled me more than you might think. Perhaps I am right in believing that your wife (to whom I addressed it) held it back to spare you unpleasantness. In that case, I hope you can read it now, because I, at least for the time being, cannot attempt to repeat the contents. The gravity of it would be too complicated—you know that I have come to take you and my feelings for you very seriously. But for me concerts, and all that they involve, are just not the most important things, and I find it difficult to recall the concerts of last winter as being vaguely anything other than pleasant.

So let me assume that the letter is still somewhere and allow me now just to add my thanks for your and the other gentlemen's greetings that cheered and honored me yesterday.

In unaltered sentiment,

J. Brahms

(BBS VIII [7], p. 34)

The birthday greetings from Bülow (and others) mentioned here by Brahms have not survived. Regarding Brahms's suspicion that Bülow's wife may have held back the letter of reconciliation, Marie von Bülow remarked, "No such letter ever reached my hands" (BBS VII [7], p. 34).

2. Johann Wolfgang von Goethe, *Egmont*, act 2, scene 2: "And of the many things I abhor, I detest writing the most."

3. Cf. letter no. 21, note 3.

4. The saying is attributed to painter Antonio Allegri, also known as Correggio (1494–1534). At seeing Raphael's painting *The Ecstasy of St. Cecilia* he is said to have exclaimed, "*Anch'io sono pittore!*" (I, too, am a painter! [Bülow: I, too, am an egoist!]).

Letter No. 30

Sign.: Mus. ep. Hans von Bülow 309. One double page, written on two sides (1r, 2r), postscript on 1v [lengthwise].

1. On 15 March 1887 in an orchestral concert in Bremen, the tenth subscription concert, advertised as taking place "in cooperation [!] with Dr. Hans von Bülow from Meiningen," Bülow conducted, among other pieces, Tragic Overture op. 81. It inspired him to the "good deed" to alleviate hardship for Carl Reinthaler (cf. note 2 below).f

2. After giving up his position in Meiningen, Bülow settled in Hamburg and accepted the position of director for subscription concerts organized by Hermann Wolff, beginning on 1 November 1886. The committee of the *Verein Bremischer Musikfreunde* (Association of Bremen's Friends of Music) asked Bülow to also conduct their subscription concerts for the season of 1887–1888. Bülow's condition was that these concert opportunities be split between himself and Carl Reinthaler. Carl (Karl) Martin Reinthaler (1822–1896) had been the municipal director of music in Bremen since 1858. In 1868 he had done everything to make the premier performance of *German Requiem* possible and managed the preparations for it. In the 1880s Reinthaler's situation in Bremen became uncomfortable; certain complaints (of dissatisfaction with his leadership and that individual singers and solo performers were privileged), left unanswered, caused the administration to try to fire him.

Brahms already knew, before receiving this letter, that the committee in Bremen intended to make Bülow the offer; the two had met in Vienna in January and February and already discussed the matter in detail (cf. BBW XI, p. 143).

3. Brahms was, as his reply indicates, well informed of the complaints against Reinthaler:

> *Esteemed Friend,*
> *I am made truly happy by your just decision and noble deed. Let's hope they will secure Reinthaler a fairly comfortable sunset for his life. Perhaps it is true that*

Reinthaler himself is more at fault—not than I know or believe—but than I care to mention and discuss.

Indeed, these dubious matters relate only to the full last 10 years of his work, and all I can add is that every single person in Bremen had a part in it. This, then leaves 20 years of which I assume from my own experience that he worked most respectably, selflessly, and diligently—battling ignorance, indifference, brutality, and foolishness—alone in this daily struggle! What do you think Richard Strauss, for instance, would look like if he were interned for 30 years in Bremen (where there's no railway connection)!

By the way, none of it is new, and none of it is anything special. It happens in every city every 20 or 30 years, it always starts and always ends the same. In Bremen it's just that the contrast between artist and Hanse town dweller is particularly sharp, or in Reinthaler's defense, let's say the contrast between the artistic and the Hanseatic.

Cordial greetings for today and the best of luck with the first of your quarter of a dozen offices! (BBS VII [7], p. 94f.)

Brahms's mention of Bülow's "quarter of a dozen offices" refers to the fact that Bülow not only conducted concerts in Hamburg and Bremen but (beginning on 12 Jan. 1887 with the performance of Bizet's *Carmen*) also conducted for Hamburg's City Theater under superintendent Bernhard Pollini (1838–1897). However, the relationship to Pollini ruptured during the 1887–1888 season. At first the Hamburg subscription concerts were given by the City Theater's orchestra (cf. letter no. 35, note 8).

4. Alludes to the previous year's "Hanusch" affair: In the autumn of 1886 Bülow had accepted an invitation by Prague's Umělecká Beseda to perform in one of her popular concerts. Remembering that when on 4 December 1884 the Meiningen orchestra played a piece by Antonín Dvořák, Bülow had announced it in the Czech language, the announcement for the 1886 Prague concert spelling Bülow's name in Czech ("Pan Dr. Hanuš z Bülowu") triggered a chauvinist campaign against Bülow in German newspapers. At a concert on 16 November 1886 in Bülow's hometown of Dresden, directly following the Prague performance, the agitation culminated in an unprecedented tumult of the audience. Bülow never again performed in Dresden. A sample of the ill humor toward Bülow is the anonymous brochure titled *Hanusch eine Reise-Vivisection: Billet-doux eines fahrenden Musikanten an seinen Freund Bartholf* [Hanusch, a Travel Vivisection: Love letter from a traveling musician to his friend Bartholf] (Vienna, 1887), playing on the title of Bülow's *Reise Recensionen* (Travel Reviews) published by Bartholf Senff.

5. Gustav Hollaender (1855–1915). As of 1881 he was concertmaster in Cologne and taught at the conservatory. He played first violin in the Cologne Quartet (consisting of Hollaender, Schwartz, Körner, and Hegyesi).

6. Daniela (cf. letter no. 12, note 6).

7. Marie von Buch (1842–1912), first married to the House of Prussia's foreign minister Count Alexander von Schleinitz, then (in 1886) to Austrian diplomat Count Anton von Wolkenstein-Trostberg, was Cosima Wagner's closest lady friend and correspondent. She was a patron of the Bayreuth Festival; to her, Wagner dedicated his essay *Das Bühnenfestspielhaus zu Bayreuth: Nebst einem Berichte über die Grundsteinlegung desselben* [The Stage Festival Hall at Bayreuth: Including a report on laying the cornerstone], in *Gesammelte Schriften und Dichtungen*, vol. 9 (Leipzig [2], 1888), p. 322ff.

8. Bülow's son-in-law, art historian Henry Thode (1857–1920). He married Daniela in 1886; they were divorced in 1914.

9. Paul Schlenther, *Frau Gottsched und die bürgerliche Komödie: Ein Kulturbild aus der Zopfzeit* (Berlin, 1886). Brahms owned a copy of the book (Hofmann, p. 103).

Letter No. 31

Sign.: Mus. ep. Hans von Bülow 310. Card without envelope, written on both sides.

1. Unknown gift. It was perhaps the book that Bülow had asked about for his daughter (see letter no. 30, note 9); after her marriage to Henry Thode, Daniela at first lived in Bonn from 1886 to 1889.

2. Unknown enclosure. It was probably a newspaper clipping regarding events involving Carl Reinthaler (see letter no. 30, note 2).

3. Klaus Groth (1819–1899), Low-German lyric and narrator, one of Brahms's friends since 1856.

4. Julius Heinrich Spengel (1853–1936), choir director for Hamburg's "Cecilia Association" and highly esteemed by both Bülow and Brahms.

5. [Maremma, a swampy coastal region in Italy.]

Letter No. 32

Sign.: Mus. ep. Hans von Bülow 311. One double page and one single page, written on five sides (1r+v, 2r+v, 3r).

1. Cello Sonata op. 99, Violin Sonata op. 100, and Piano Trio op. 101.

2. Rudolf von Beckerath (1833–1888), winery owner in Rüdesheim, known to Brahms as of 1874 and friends with him as of 1880.

3. Cécile Mutzenbecher (1849–1907), née Gorrison, probably met Bülow in 1886 in Hamburg where she was staying with her parents for 1886–1887. After divorce from her husband, merchant Gustav Mutzenbecher from Hamburg, she resided in Wiesbaden. Her daughter Mathilde took up piano lessons in 1885–1886 with Clara Schumann at the Hoch Conservatory. In November 1889 Bülow's wife's jealousy caused him to break off his

relationship to Cécile Mutzenbecher. The area "Nerotal" mentioned in the letter is adjacent to Wiesbaden's northern neighborhood of villas.

4. To which must be added χαλά (πάντα λίαυ χαλά), meaning, "And God saw that *it was* good," from the first book of Moses (Genesis 1:10, 12, 18, 21, 25, and 31).

5. Fritz Simrock.

6. Theodor Kirchner (cf. letter no. 49, note 4). Bülow is here alluding to the last verse of Goethe's poem "Dinner in Koblenz in the Summer of 1774": "Prophets to the right, prophets to the left, / The worldling in between."

Regarding his trip to Italy with Simrock and Kirchner, Brahms wrote to Bülow,

> *I had been very happy about Simrock's kind idea of letting Kirchner take a look at the beautiful country. But I'm afraid the idea came twenty years too late. It seemed that he never felt quite comfortable until punctually at lunch or dinner he could again talk about the concert hall and similar grand things.* (Kalbeck 4/1, p. 44f.)

7. Cf. letter no. 30, note 4.

8. Frits Hartvigson (1841–1919), pianist and piano teacher in London as of 1864. From 1859 to 1861 he had been Bülow's piano student at the Stern Conservatory in Berlin.

9. Cf. letter no. 27, note 7.

10. "Mrs. Mutzenbecher as Raphael's original" means the painting *The Ecstasy of St. Cecelia* by Raphael Sanzio (1483–1520) in Bologna's Pinacoteca Nazionale (National Art Gallery).

11. George Gordon Noel (Lord of) Byron (1788–1824) left England in 1816 and at first lived in Switzerland, then in Italy, which he fled in 1823 for political reasons. Shortly after his arrival in Greece, where he had gone to participate in the Greek War of Independence from the Ottoman Empire, he died of malaria. His major works (the end of *Childe Harold's Pilgrimage*, as well as *Manfred* and *Cain*) were written in Italy.

12. Author Giosuè Carducci (1835–1907), particularly known for his lyrics, was professor for the history of literature in Bologna from 1861 until 1903. In 1906 he was awarded the Nobel Prize for Literature.

13. Carl Heinrich Carsten Reinecke (1824–1910). In 1859–1860 he conducted the Breslau Sing Academy; as of 1860 he was conductor at Leipzig's *Gewandhaus* concerts.

As of 1860 Julius Schaeffer (1823–1902) was musical director at the university and (succeeding Reinecke) the conductor at the Breslau Sing Academy.

The three music festivals that Bülow mentions here are (1) the Lower Rhine Music Festival in Dusseldorf (29–31 May 1887), where (directed by Hans Richter) Brahms's Academic Festival Overture op. 80 was performed on

May 31; (2) the Silesian Music Festival in Breslau (5–7 June 1887), where Carl Reinecke was a guest conductor; and (3) the Musician's Festival of the General German Music Association (Allgemeiner Deutscher Musikverein [ADMV]) in Cologne (26–29 June 1887). The fact that Brahms for the first time ever participated in an ADMV music festival was considered a minor sensation (see note 16 below).

14. Theodor Kirchner.

15. After marrying Henry Thode, Bülow's daughter Daniela first lived in Bonn, where her husband, who at that time was working toward the *venia legendi* (permission for lecturing) in art history, was employed by the university (from 1886 to 1889).

16. Brahms played his new Piano Trio in C minor op. 101 more or less on the side at the ADMV Musician's Festival on the afternoon of 28 June 1887. For his reply to Bülow, see letter no. 33, note 1.

17. Alludes to the opus number of the trio in C minor.

Letter No. 33

Sign.: Mus. ep. Hans von Bülow 312. One double page, written on two sides (1r, 2r).

1. Heinrich Zöllner (1854–1941), *Faust*, opera in four acts, premier performance on 19 October 1887 in Munich. Brahms had answered Bülow's question from letter no. 32 (note 16) as follows:

> *Yes, dear friend, I write this with a sigh, I suppose I must keep my promise to Wüllner and attend Cologne. I'm not involved in the actual festival, I will only be playing my trio on the evening beforehand (school choir performance). I don't look forward to the music business, but I should and would like the prospects of traveling along the Rhine and visiting the many lovely places, if only there weren't so many, and the cellars weren't so cool and pleasant!*
>
> *From Cologne, incidentally, comes the most outrageous novelty of all times: Zöllner's "Faust." I'm at a lack of words for it, but I shall never again say worse things about Gounod and Boito. A boy will place tragedies by Sophocles and Shakespeare on his piano rack and hammer and howl his enthusiasm to the heights. But to me it was a crime, a sin, when once a very young man brought me a score he had written for the dungeon scene; to me it testified against the whole person and artist. What if one as uneducated and crazy as Bruckner had done that! But no, a respectable, learned man ponders and works on it for years, sits his bare a— down on a sanctum and sh—s and works on it. It's not ridiculous, it's scandalous and utterly inexcusable.* (Kalbeck 4/1, p. 48)

2. Kölner Männer-Gesangverein (Cologne's men's choir association). Zöllner had been its conductor since 1885.

3. Franz Wüllner's address.

4. Bismarck's second oldest son Wilhelm Otto Albrecht, nicknamed Billi (1852–1901). From 1882 to 1885 he was member of the Prussian House of Representatives; in 1885 he became district administrator for Hanau, in 1889 district president for Hanover, and ultimately in 1895 district president for East Prussia.

5. [The Bismarck herring is traditionally served with a bun. Bülow is saying that the younger Bismarck is not the fish, he's just the bun. CK]

6. Walter Johannes Damrosch (1862–1950) was conductor at the Metropolitan Opera in New York as of 1884. In the 1850s and 1860s Bülow had artistically worked closely with Walter's father, Leopold Damrosch (1832–1885), who immigrated to New York in 1871.

7. The enclosure has not survived. It must have been a newspaper article reporting Reinthaler's retirement that was officially announced on 24 May 1887 and that put an end to Bülow's efforts to get Reinthaler reintegrated into Bremen's concert scene (cf. letter no. 30). But it did not put an end to Bülow's efforts for Reinthaler in Bremen altogether: On 9 December 1887 at a benefit concert for the orchestra's pension fund, Bülow let Reinthaler conduct the first half of the program, while he conducted the second half, and on 29 December 1888 Bülow opened a concert for the pension fund with a performance of Reinthaler's "Edda" Overture.

8. Regarding "crock devotees," see Bülow's letter to daughter Daniela, dated 29 March 1887: "I'll attend the music festival in Cologne, but stay in Bonn (Hotel Royal). It's wonderful to escape the musical mob's tavern-going by buying one-day round-trip train tickets" (*New Letters*, p. 648).

9. Cécile Mutzenbecher.

Letter No. 34

Sign.: Mus. ep. Hans von Bülow 313. One double page, written on one side (1r).

1. Joseph Joachim (cf. letter no. 12, note 7) and Robert Hausmann (1852–1909) were the two soloists in the Berlin performance of the Double Concerto op. 102 at the sixth philharmonic concert on 6 February 1888. As of 1876 Hausmann taught at the Royal College for Music in Berlin; as of 1879 he was cellist in Joachim's string quartet.

2. Between this letter and the next, Brahms received a congratulatory telegram from Wiesbaden (dated 7 May 1888) in which Bülow was also involved: "May [our] highly esteemed Master be congratulated from our whole hearts on a new year of his life, on the condition that he makes the same

the year of birth of Symphony no. 5, or as one of us—Bülow—would say, Symphony no. 14. Cécile Mutzenbecher" (taken from Kalbeck 4/1, p. 117).

Letter No. 35

Sign.: Mus. ep. Hans von Bülow 314. One double page, written on four sides (1r+v, 2r+v).

1. Louise Salingré (Salinger), first wife of pianist Eugen d'Albert. She married d'Albert in 1884; they were divorced in 1890. Louise d'Albert-Salingré then lived a secluded life at Lake Starnberg until her death in 1929.

2. The message mentioned is Brahms's reaction to a (no longer extant) packet sent by Bülow: Bülow had opened the concert season in Berlin on 15 October 1888 with the first philharmonic concert by putting, among other things, Brahms's Haydn Variations op. 56a on the program. Two days later, on 17 October 1888 in Hamburg, Bülow performed Brahms's Piano Sonata op. 1 at a chamber music soirée given by the Bargheer Quartet. He sent Brahms a copy of the printed program, on which, as Brahms's reply indicates, he had written a note, probably making reference to the andante movement. Brahms replied,

> *Getting your program and the note was a real joy. And although they at first stirred nostalgic sentiments, they then reminded me of when I first so earnestly felt and wrote those words and notes. I felt strong and confident, and I now dearly wish that you feel the same.—Just as I put my pen aside and was thinking of you, a letter arrived from S. He writes, among other things, "The Variations went wonderfully—you're familiar with Bülow's interpretation and performance, it is spirited, fine, and beautiful—down to the last dot." Upon reading such dignified (!), splendid words, I put my pen down again, but my thoughts wander happily to the lovely Alster Basin and to you. Send me another program soon—with another wonderful note!* (Kalbeck 1/1, p. 157)

3. Brahms returns to this phrase in his next letter:

> *It's natural for a letter to arrive a* tempo *for you, for you every day is a Sunday or concert day; but neither is it difficult for a letter to be a* tempissimo, *if it means that one of my pieces will be part of your program. That reminds me of your recent talk on my Sonata in C major. And that takes me back further yet and reminds me that you were the first to play one of my pieces publicly. It was this sonata, and it was in Hamburg, too, at a concert given by Mrs. Peroni-Glassbrenner. I easily found the year 1853 in Simrock's catalog. The sonata had not even been published yet, you had gotten yourself a copy of it and played it by memory.*
>
> *All of this shows that I have hardly changed with the passage of time. You tease me because I care little about publicity. It's not something that developed, it*

Postcard view of the Alster Basin. *Courtesy of Cynthia Klohr*

has always been that way. I can't ask that you really understand it, otherwise you would not be our indispensable Hans v. Bülow. But from the fact that I, who have never kept a diary, stored those events deep in my heart, you must realize or sense that even my dread of the public has its limits. I have always been destined for the monastery—except that the right kind does not exist. (Kalbeck 1/1, p. 157 f.)

The first public (partial) performance of the sonata was on 1 March 1854, when Bülow played the first movement only. It is unclear whether Bülow really learned the piece from "a copy," as Brahms believes to recall, because the sonata was published in December 1853, shortly before Bülow met Brahms for the first time.

4. Henrik Ibsen (1828–1906), *An Enemy of the People*, act 5: By exclaiming "Indeed, if you knew how things are around here," print shop owner Aslaksen sums up the bigotry, intrigues, and opportunism governing the communal policy of the little bath resort where the play takes place. Bülow liked using the phrase.

The Haydn Variations op. 56a were part of a motley program (Hamburg, 11 Nov. 1888, second subscription concert) that (in contrast to the Philharmonic concerts in Berlin) were thoroughly typical of Bülow's first years in Hamburg and Bremen (thus his allusion to local circumstances). It contained the Corsair Overture by Berlioz, Violin Concerto op. 87 by Ed. Lassen, the scene for a baritone from Philipp von Artevelde by F. A. Gevaert, the Haydn Variations by J. Brahms, Sonnet and Chant de Mai by G. Huberti, and Symphony in C major by F. Schubert.

5. Cf. letter no. 24, note 3.

6. Hamburg, 10 January 1889 (fourth subscription concert).

7. Theodor Avé-Lallement (1806–1884), member of the board of the Hamburg Philharmonic Committee.

8. Julius Von Bernuth (1830–1902), as of 1873 director of the Hamburg Conservatory founded by him, also director of Hamburg's "philharmonic concerts."

The long imminent conflict between Bernuth and Bülow broke out when Bülow, whose concerts (organized by Hermann Wolff) had always been performed by the City Theater Orchestra, had to set up an entirely new orchestra for the third season of "new subscription concerts" because the theater's orchestra was no longer at his disposal after he resigned from the opera (cf. letter no. 30, note 3). Backed by the Philharmonic Committee, Bernuth forbade the members of his orchestra (many of whom lacked contracts and were engaged only from time to time) to participate in Bülow's concerts. Despite this measure, frowned upon by the majority of Hamburg's concertgoers, Bülow was able to form a new orchestra to present the "new subscription concerts."

9. On Brodsky, see letter no. 27, note 3.

In reaction to Bernuth's boycott initiative, Brodsky, professor at the Leipzig Conservatory as of 1882, spontaneously agreed to participate gratuitously—as a member of the orchestra—in all Bülow concerts. For the first five (of six) concerts during the season of 1888/89 he played second violin in the new orchestra. The back of the printed programs listing all members of the orchestra notes explicitly, "Prof. A. Brodsky from Leipzig, guest of honor." Brodsky's gesture was of considerable significance to Hamburg's orchestra musicians.

10. Julius Klengel (1859–1933), solo cellist at Leipzig's Gewandhaus Orchestra and, as of 1881, like Brodsky, professor at the Leipzig Conservatory.

11. Cf. Double Concerto op. 102, first movement, measure 5.

12. On 7 February 1889, the fifth subscription concert did not include the Academic Festival Overture after all, but closed instead with Symphony no. 3 (see note 14 below).

13. On 22 February 1889 at the sixth subscription concert, Bülow played Piano Concerto no. 1, op. 15, conducted by Adolph Brodsky, not by Spengel.

14. The "Special Benefit Concert for the Members of the Orchestra" (9 March 1889) included two works by Brahms (both conducted by him): Symphony no. 4, op. 98, and the Academic Festival Overture op. 80. (Symphony no. 3 had been moved to the fifth subscription concert; see note 12 above).

15. Ignaz Brüll (1846–1907), *Das Steinerne Herz*, a fairy-tale opera (1888). Brüll belonged to the inner circle of Brahms's friends in Vienna. In 1882 he (and Theodor Billroth) accompanied Brahms on the latter's third trip to Italy.

16. The co-wagon drivers, in other words, propagandists for Brahms (see letter no. 24, note 3), were Eduard Hanslick (from the *Neue Freie Presse*) and Max Kalbeck (at the *Presse*).

Letter No. 36

Sign.: Mus. Ep. Hans von Bülow 315. One double page, written on three sides (1r+v, 2r).

1. On 30 January the newspapers had reported the death of Archduke Rudolph, the Austrian successor to the throne.

2. The two soloists performing the Double Concerto op. 102 in Bremen on 29 January 1889 were Ernst Skalitzky (violin) and Wilhelm Kufferath (cello). Ernst Hugo Robert Skalitzky (1853–1926), one of Joseph Joachim's pupils, had been concertmaster of the Bremen Orchestra as of 1879.

Bülow's deep appreciation for Skalitzky and Kufferath can be seen in the fact that he asked them to again perform Brahms's Double Concerto as soloists at the fifth Hamburg subscription concert of the season 1889/90. Among Bülow's remaining papers we find the printed program from this concert on which Bülow commented on the performance of the Double Concerto as being "excellent" and, particularly regarding the finale, "da Capo demanded!" (SBB, Sign.: Db 1815 [5]).

3. Joseph Joachim.

4. Hans Richter performed Joachim's overture (see note 5) on 16 December 1888 at the second concert of the Society of the Friends of Music in Vienna. Cf. also Hanslick's review of that concert in Eduard Hanslick, *Musikalisches und Litterarisches*, Der "Modernen Oper" VI. Theil (Berlin [3] 1892), pp. 256–258.

5. Joseph Joachim had composed his Orchestra Overture op. 13, "dedicated to the memory of the poet Heinrich von Kleist" in 1876 in gratitude for receiving an honorary doctorate degree from Cambridge University. The premier performance was on 8 March 1877 in Cambridge at the conferral ceremony. Bülow put the overture at the top of the program of the seventh philharmonic concert in Berlin on 21 January 1889. He had had it performed once before, on 26 April 1878 during his first season in Hanover, where Joseph and Amalie Joachim played the solo parts.

6. Hanslick and Kalbeck.

7. Hanslick's detailed review of the Double Concerto op. 102 performed in Vienna on 23 December 1888 by the Philharmonic directed by Hans Richter (Joachim and Hausmann playing the solos) was unexpectedly negative: "I am sorry enough to have to admit that it [the new work] did not provide the great pleasure that earlier great works by Brahms have given"; at any rate

the piece does not belong "among the best of Brahms's creations" Eduard Hanslick, *Musikalisches und Litterarisches*, Der "Modernen Oper" V. Theil (Berlin [3] 1890), pp. 149–156.

8. In reviewing Brahms's *Lieder* booklets that appeared in October and November 1888, op. 105, op. 106, and op. 107, Hanslick had exuberantly welcomed the "new *Lieder* as one of the most valuable Christmas gifts" and discussed their qualities in detail (Hanslick, as in note 7, pp. 142–149).

Letter No. 37

Sign.: Mus. ep. Hans von Bülow 317. One double page, written on three sides (1r+v, 2r).

1. About the date: In BBS VIII (7), p. 255, this letter is indexed erroneously because its indication of being written on St. John's Day (*Johannistag*) 1889 misleadingly makes it appear to have been written on 24 June (summer solstice). But that order is impossible, because Brahms's reply is dated 30 May and Bülow's confirmation of receiving Brahms's reply is dated 4 June (see letter no. 38). The reason for writing "St. John's Day" was another: Bülow is playing on the coincidental identity the date shares with that of the announcement that Johannes Brahms has been made an honorary citizen of the city of Hamburg, implying a considerable rise in status (see note 2). Bülow wrote a letter of thanks on the same day to the daughter of Hamburg's mayor (Wiesbaden, 24 May 1889; BBS VIII [7], p. 251f.). He waited for the announcement of Brahms's honorary citizenship before thanking Brahms for dedicating Violin Sonata op. 108 to him.

2. Brahms's "rise in status" refers to him being made an "honorary citizen" of the city of Hamburg. He was informed by telegram on 23 May.

The dedication printed in Violin Sonata op. 108 published in April 1889 reads, "Dedicated [by the composer] to his friend Hans von Bülow."

3. Carl Friedrich Petersen (1809–1892), mayor of Hamburg, whom Bülow won over for the idea of awarding Brahms the title of honorary citizen. It had been Bülow's idea from the start, but he remained in the background throughout the entire decision-making process (that was not readily accepted by Hamburg's citizenry).

4. Found among Brahms's remaining papers in the archive of the Society of the Friends of Music in Vienna. Brahms's own handwritten list of his musical belongings includes these two birthday gifts from Bülow: François-Adrien Boieldieu (1775–1834), piano scores from "Red Riding Hood (French and German) Br. and H." and "*Les voitures versées* (French) Paris" (Hofmann, p. 24).

5. A music shop established in 1795 in Hamburg by Johann August Böhme.

6. Bertha Von Dewitz. In 1883 Brahms spent the summer at her villa in Wiesbaden (from 20 May to 3 October 1883). An attempt to repeat that stay the next year failed because Brahms asked too late whether it was still available (cf. BBW XIII, p. 118f.).

Cécile Mutzenbecher regretted that after Mrs. von Dewitz died (30 Nov. 1886), Brahms had little reason and opportunity to spend the greater part of the summer in Wiesbaden.

7. Theodor Billroth (1829–1894), from 1860 to 1867 professor for surgery in Zurich, as of 1867 surgeon and university professor in Vienna, a close friend of Brahms as of 1866.

8. Brahms replied on 30 May 1889:

Dear Friend,

over the past few days I have written the loveliest letters to our mayor and today I sent the most wretched of them! You see, this so unexpected but really wonderful distinction easily lets me ramble on and on . . . but none of it has anything to do with the mayor himself, so in the end I have nothing to write him.

I would never have fancied it, but then again, it's not my habit to dream of awards, and it feels much different than I thought—although, the main part is missing. I wish my dear father could have lived to see it; to see him happy would have made me so very happy.

I will do my best not to forget July 6, but who besides you always has the calendar in mind and at hand!

But now (having written so many letters in vain) let me candidly make a simple request with the sincere plea that you consider and treat it frankly. I have, namely, a suitable piece for your music festival, if the circumstances favor it:

Three short, hymnlike pieces for an eight-part a cappella choir, appropriate for national festive and commemoration days, to mention Leipzig, Sedan, and coronations explicitly. (No, better not!)

For your particular case they would be quite good, but you would have to consider what might not work: the hall is perhaps not appropriate, there may not be enough time for choir practice, it would depend on the other items on the program, etc. The pieces are not very difficult, I guess you could add horns, on day two for example that might make a nice change of sound, but consider all the points just mentioned.

It occurs to me that I could just send the choir parts with this letter! So that's what I'll do, and since I don't know your exact [present] address, please send me a card saying whether this letter and the roll have arrived!

Once again, be honest and tell me any objections.

Boieldieu hasn't reached me yet, but I thank you for it and for your nice letter. (I was relieved that you like the sonata.)

But now I would like to go for a walk and since I can't walk to the Nero Mountain, please at least greet your wife and Mrs. Cecilia. Cordially, your J. Brahms. (Kalbeck 4/1, p. 183f.; "Mrs. Cecilia" is Cécile Mutzenbecher.)

Letter No. 38

Sign.: Mus. ep. Hans von Bülow 316. One double page, written on two sides (1r, 2r).

1. Festival and Commemoration Pieces, Four Songs for an Eight-Part Chorus (a cappella), op. 109; in gratitude for the title of honorary citizen of the city of Hamburg. Brahms dedicated them "in reverence" to "His Magnificence, Mayor Dr. Carl Petersen in Hamburg." Brahms sent the manuscript; they were not printed until February 1890.

2. Cf. letter no. 37, note 5.

3. Cf. letter no. 31, note 4.

4. Cf. letter no. 32, note 3.

5. Laura von Beckerath, née Deus (1840–1921), spouse of Rudolf von Beckerath (cf. letter no. 32, note 2).

6. The enclosure has not survived; possibly a newspaper clipping.

Letter No. 39

Sign.: Mus. ep. Hans von Bülow 318. One double page, written on four sides (1r+v, 2r+v).

*Villeggiatura: summer resort, pun on the German word *Tür* (doorway).

1. *Senf(f) geben* (literally, add mustard): to give one's unsolicited opinion; a play on *Signals for the World of Music* edited by Leipzig's publisher Bartholf Senff.

2. Brahms did attend the three festive concerts on 9, 11, and 13 September 1889 that Bülow had arranged for the opening of Hamburg's Industrial Exhibition. In the first of the three concerts, the Cäcilien Association, directed by Julius Spengel, gave the premier performance of Brahms's Festival and Commemoration Pieces op. 109.

3. See letter no. 35, note 4.

4. Arnold Krug (1849–1904), as of 1885 instructor at Hamburg's conservatory and director of the *Altona Singverein*.

5. Georg Hulbe (1851–1917), bookbinder and applied craftsman, established in Hamburg as of 1880, ran a workshop having eventually two hundred employees. While Hulbe was entrusted with decorating for the ceremony, Hamburg's painter and sculptor Paul Duyffke (1847–1910, as of 1872 teacher at Hamburg's vocational school) was asked to design the certificate of honorary citizenship.

6. Bülow's attitude toward Giuseppe Verdi (1813–1901) changed several times. Characteristic of his phase of severest disapproval during the 1870s and 1880s is the article "Musikalisches aus Italien" [Musical Remarks from Italy] written in May 1874 for the *Allgemeine Zeitung*, where he calls Verdi "the

omnipotent corruptor of Italian artistic taste" (BBS III/2, p. 136), a quip for which Bülow in 1892 asked Verdi to forgive him, calling it a "*gran bestialitá giornalistica*" [a huge journalistic blunder].

Bolko Graf von Hochberg (1843–1926), composer of several instrumental and stage pieces, was, as of 1886, general superintendent of the royal theater in Berlin and as such was also responsible for Bülow's expulsion from Berlin's opera house on 28 February 1887 (see letter no. 40, note 7). In a letter to the board of Bonn's Beethoven House dated 29 June 1889, Bülow turned down the offer of honorary membership in the association, saying that he "did not wish to see [his] name on a list that includes that of Graf von Hochberg" (BBS VIII [7], p. 257f.).

Alphons Czibulka (1842–1894), composer of dance music and operettas, was an army orchestra director in Vienna.

Victor Ernst Nessler (1841–1890) became known predominantly for his opera *Der Trompeter von Säckingen* [The Trumpeter of Saeckingen] (1884).

Contrary to Bülow, in May 1889 Brahms accepted honorary membership to Bonn's Beethoven House Association.

7. Ferdinand Hiller.

8. Address of Brahms's birthplace in Hamburg.

Letter No. 40

Sign.: Mus. ep. Hans von Bülow 319. One double page, written on two sides (1r+v), postscript on 2v, 2r: printed declaration against Wilhelm Tappert (cf. note 7 below).

1. *Gekesselter Trompeteus*: a play on Karl Goldmark's (1830–1915) overture to "*Der gefesselte Prometheus*" that (under Goldmark's direction) was performed for the first time in Bülow's concert of 25 November 1889 (fourth philharmonic concert).

2. Exodus 24:11 (see also letter no. 42, note 1).

3. The enclosure has not survived. It seems to have been reviews written by Ludwig Speidel that Brahms sent to Bülow without any further comment. In reply to Bülow's letter no. 40, Brahms wrote,

> *In order that my mail today does not get by without a word (being lazy, I have done it too often), let me say in afterthought that this is only meant as a sign of how pleased I was by your most recent kind, good, and beautiful words. They touched my heart so truly and kindly that I cannot decide whether to send you any more Speidel* [clippings] . . . , *Lovingly, your J. Br.* (Taken from Geiringer, p. 163f.)

4. On Elisabeth von Herzogenberg, see letter no. 10, note 11. She and her husband, composer Heinrich von Herzogenberg (1841–1900), were among the most competent and appreciative judges of Brahms's music.

5. The program for the fifth subscription concert in Hamburg on 12 December 1889 included the Double Concerto op. 102. Ernst Skalitzky and Wilhelm Kufferath played the solos (see letter no. 36, note 2).

6. When trying to convince his friend Hans von Bronsart to acknowledge Brahms's symphonies (3 August 1888; BBS VIII [7], p. 206), Bülow had used the phrase "latent warmth" to describe Brahms's music. Bronsart replied, "Precisely *latent* warmth *is* characteristic of Brahms's indeed highly significant individuality. Latent warmth is one of the most interesting and important doctrines of physics; but latent warmth is incapable of achieving any *direct* effect (even heating a stove), and I believe that in art The Ultimate and The Greatest . . . is that which works directly" (BBS VIII [7], p. 208f.).

7. Refers to paper that Bülow used as stationery for several letters in November and December 1889. One half of the sheet was a printed attack on Wilhelm Tappert.

In supplement no. 280 to the newspaper *General News for Hamburg Altona* dated 28 November 1889, Berlin's musicologist and critic Wilhelm Tappert (1830–1907) had written an article titled "Eight Days in Hamburg: Musical Small Talk by Wilhelm Tappert (Berlin)" mentioning the prehistory of Bülow's being expelled from Berlin's opera house in February 1887, namely, the so-called "Circus Hülsen Affair" that had actually taken place a whole five years previously.

At a Berlin concert on 4 March 1884, Bülow had addressed the audience and called the royal opera "Circus Hülsen" after its superintendent Botho von Hülsen. That statement led to Bülow's loss of the title of pianist for the house of Prussia, documented by a decree signed on 10 April 1884 by imperial secretary of state Graf von Schleinitz. On the reverse side of that document Bülow had drafted an extremely sarcastic riposte, concluding by saying that he was glad

> to know that my name no longer figures among the circle of exceedingly dubious subjects at a court whose artistic ambition can only compete with that of his former majesty, the [Zulu] king of Cetewayo.

Bülow's reply remained a draft and was never sent. But he gave Schleinitz's letter, with his own reaction sketched on the back, to someone and unfortunately it became known. This probably inclined Hülsen's successor Hochberg to have Bülow ushered out of the foyer of Berlin's opera house on 28 February 1887 (Bülow had tickets to see the première of Philippe Rüfer's *Merlin*).

Tappert's feuilleton article quotes Bülow's reply as if the draft were an official letter found among Graf Schleinitz's remaining papers (he had died on 19 February 1885). Bülow defended himself by using a printed counterstatement as stationery, hoping that Hamburg's local press would correct the misinformation (see letter no. 43, note 4).

The counterstatement reads as follows:

Disappointment.

To the disclosure by Mr. Wilhelm Tappert in his feuilleton article "Eight Days in Hamburg" concerning the prehistory of my expulsion from the Berlin Opera House, I retort:

I shall immediately pay ten thousand marks in cash to "Mr. Robert and Mr. Bertram" (see German Stage Almanac, Altenburg Royal Theater) as a pittance to relieve the deficit caused by the next Silesian music . . . festival as soon as anyone can produce the "official file" that supposedly proves these events. Granted, dear Almarica: there is no fiction without truth. The truth is that on the back of the "Decree Suspending the Title of Imperial Pianist," sent to me in Meiningen on 10 April 1884, I scribbled my reply quoted by Mr. Tappert solely for my own pleasure. Shortly afterward I lost the document to someone who collects autographs. However, that sketch remained a "draft" (Brouillon); it never became clean copy, and thus was never sent to the intended address. Ergo, the late secretary of the House [of Prussia] never received it as a "letter" and it cannot have been found among his estate.

Hamburg, late November 1889
Dr. Hans von Bülow

Letter No. 41

Sign.: Mus. Ep. Hans von Bülow 327. Card without envelope, written on both sides.

1. The date: To celebrate Ludwig van Beethoven's 119th birthday (see the closing of the letter), Bülow directed on 16 December 1889 a concert with the Berlin Philharmonic Choir (music from the *Festspiel* "The Ruins of Athens," Symphony no. 9, op. 125, with choir finale).

2. There exists no "Achilleis" for Aeschylus; Bülow is perhaps playing on the first part of Goethe's "Achilleis" fragment (verse 7ff.).

3. The enclosure has not survived; it has not been possible to determine who is meant.

4. Anton Bruckner and Ignaz Brüll.

5. Anton Schindler (1798–1864), a friend of Beethoven's as of 1814; as of 1816 and until Beethoven's death, Schindler was Beethoven's secretary and companion.

Letter No. 42

Sign.: Mus. ep. Hans von Bülow 320. One page, written on both sides.

1. Bülow's indication of source is not quite correct; he means his favorite Bible verse: "They saw God, and did eat and drink" (Exodus 24:11); see also letter no. 40, note 2, and letter no. 55, note 1.

2. Refers to Brahms's Violin Sonata op. 108 (dedicated to Bülow) and the "beautiful edition" of Symphony no. 2, op. 73 (not found in Bülow's estate).

3. For issue no. 18 in vol. 3, 1889/90, of the *Hamburgische Musikzeitung* (Hamburg Journal of Music) published by Johann August Böhme Verlag, Bülow had written an article dated "Hamburg, Christmas 1889" titled "Dr. Shohé Tanaka's Enharmonic," praising in detail the Japanese's invention of a perfect-pitched harmonium having twenty-one notes per octave. The instrument, he said, respects "the gospel of the purity of musical art as established by the laws of nature." To this he added polemics against well-tempered tuning, an "admittedly practically indispensable, but none the less conventional *piano lie*." Within this context, Bülow cited an explicitly orally conveyed thought of Brahms's: "Today we can no longer compose as beautifully as Mozart did, but what we can do is to try to compose as clearly as he did" (BBS III/2, p. 253). For Brahms's correction of the quote see letter no. 48, note 1.

4. Here Bülow uses the name Speidel as representative of the type of music critic he hated. The reference is to a concert at the Leipzig Gewandhaus on 28 November 1889 performing Karl Goldmark's "Der Gefesselte Prometheus" [Prometheus in Chains], an overture not to its missing last part, but to the first part of Aeschylus's "Prometheia." A concert review in the *New Journal for Music*, however, distorted the name of the piece, saying that on 28 November Goldmark had emerged "with a new manuscript overture to *The Unchained Prometheus* by Aeschylus"; *Neue Zeitschrift für Musik* 56 (1889): p. 565 (14 Dec. 1889).

In this letter Bülow mentions only the events in Leipzig, although a remarkably similar thing happened in Berlin: On 25 November 1889, a few days prior to the Gewandhaus concert, Bülow and the Berlin Philharmonic had performed the première of Goldmark's overture (directed by the composer). The concert announcement in the *Neue Berliner Musikzeitung* [Berlin's New Journal of Music] 43 (1889): p. 320 (26. Sept. 1889) called the piece—just as mistakenly as the review from Leipzig—"Carl Goldmark's newest, not yet published overture to Aeschylus' *Unchained Prometheus*."

5. "Newspaper lice" (*Fremdenblattläuse*) is a pun on *Fremdenblatt* (Foreign News, the Viennese newspaper for which music critic Ludwig Speidel wrote articles), combining it with *Blattlaus* (plant louse) to denote unfavorable critics. The newspaper clippings Bülow sent to encourage Brahms not to cease sending him reviews by Speidel have not survived.

Letter No. 43

Sign.: Mus. ep. Hans von Bülow 321. One double page, written on three sides (1r+v, 2r).

1. See letter no. 24, note 3.

2. Eduard Hanslick and Max Kalbeck.

3. Hamburg's publisher Hugo Pohle (publisher of Carl Goldmark's opera *The Queen of Saba*, op. 27; Goldmark's opera *Merlin* was published without an opus number by Julius Schuberth in Leipzig) was the editor of the *Hamburg Signals* that appeared every two weeks ("*almost* monthly"). The name of the publication followed that of the renowned *Signals for the World of Music* edited by Bartholf Senff (Leipzig). Pohle had printed a call protesting the award of honorary citizenship to Brahms and circulated it among Hamburg's prominent citizens.

4. Within the context of the counterstatement to Tappert's feuilleton article of 28 November 1889 (see letter no. 40, note 7), Bülow let the charges he successfully pressed against Wilhelm Tappert (1887, mentioned in this letter as exemplary punishment for Tappert's Brahms critiques) appear to be the chief motivation for Tappert's invective against him. In the newspaper *Hamburgische Correspondent* (2 Dec. 1889), Bülow relates the episode as follows: "Some years ago, Mr. Tappert and Mr. von Bülow were such good acquaintances that the 'critic' asked the virtuoso for a loan of 600 marks and got it. As the date determined for repayment had passed and gentle reminders were of no avail, Mr. von Bülow, as immediate sources report, found it necessary to consult a Berlin lawyer on the matter. In kindness, the debtor was given three months to repay the sum, and when that did not occur, legal measures were taken. Mr. Tappert had to pay and Mr. von Bülow donated the entire sum to health insurance for the Association of Berlin's Music Instructors, sending it to the chairman of the board, Mr. Oscar Eichberg."

On 17 March 1887 the *New Berlin Journal of Music* reported Bülow's donation of twice the sum involved in the incident, namely 1,200 marks, to the Berlin Association of Music Instructors (Berliner Musiklehrer-Verein).

5. Dante Alighieri (1265–1321), *Divine Comedy: Inferno*, third song, verses 49–51: "*Fama di loro il mondo esser non lassa, / Misericordia e Giustizia li sdegna; / Non ragionam di lor, ma guarda e passa.*"

6. Bülow's article about the Enharmonium (see letter no. 42, note 3). His joking request for amnesty refers to his unauthorized use of Brahms's quotation (for Brahms's reaction to that request see letter no. 48, note 1).

Letter No. 44

Sign.: Mus. ep. Hans von Bülow 322. One double page, written on two sides (1r+v), on 2r: the published statement opposing Wilhelm Tappert (see letter no. 40, note 4).

1. Heinrich Heine (1797–1856), *Buch der Lieder* ("Lyrisches Intermezzo"), 33: "Ein Fichtenbaum steht einsam / Im Norden auf kahler Höh. / Ihm schläfert; mit weißer Decke / Umhüllen ihn Eis und Schnee."

Lieder Book ("Lyrical Intermezzo"), 33: "A sole spruce tree stands / in the north at bleak height, / lulled by ice and snow / that wrap him in white."

2. Anton Rubinstein (1829–1894; "from P." = from Petersburg). Rubinstein composed several pieces explicitly designated as "sacred operas." By "sweeping away" memories of Rubinstein with the "valiant seventy-threes," Bülow means his performance of Beethoven's Piano Concerto no. 5, op. 73 (soloist: Bülow), and Brahms's Symphony no. 2, op. 73, at the Königsberg Orchestra Concert on 16 January 1890 (Wagner, Beethoven, Brahms, Moszkowski, Berlioz). On the next day (17 Jan. 1890) Bülow gave a piano soirée with a mixed program.

3. Pianist and composer Woldemar Bargiel (1828–1897), Clara Schumann's stepbrother, as of 1874 professor at Berlin's College of Music. On Heinrich von Herzogenberg see letter no. 40, note 4. Ernst Friedrich Karl Rudorff (1840–1916) was one of Bargiel's students; as of 1869 he was professor at Berlin's College of Music and as of 1880 director of the Stern Singing Association. He was also involved in preparing complete editions of Mozart and Chopin. Ferdinand Thieriot (1838–1919) had in Hamburg been a pupil of Brahms's teacher Eduard Marxsen. At the time this letter was written he was artistic director of the Steiermark Music Association in Graz (until 1895).

4. The members of Königsberg's "Brahms Community" are as follows, in the order Bülow mentions them: Johannes von Mikulicz-Radecki (1850–1905), from 1875 to 1878 was student and then from 1878 to 1881 assistant under Theodor Billroth in Vienna, as of 1882 professor and director of the surgical clinic in Crakow; as of 1887 he held the same position in Königsberg and then finally in the spring of 1890 in Breslau. Ludimar Herrmann (1838–1914), was as of 1868 professor for physiology in Zurich; as of 1884 he held the same position in Königsberg; in 1892/93 he was rector of the University of Königsberg. Gustav Hirschfeld (1847–1895), an archeologist, directed excavations in Olympia in 1874 when Praxiteles' Hermes was discovered; as of 1878 he was adjunct professor and as of 1882 professor in ordinary at Königsberg. Alexander Wyneken (1848–1939) as of 1876 was employee and as of 1886 chief editor at the *Königsberger Allgemeine Zeitung*. Therese Simon, née Kusserow, was married in her second marriage to merchant and Swiss consul Gustav Simon and lived as of 1879 in Königsberg.

5. Brahms had sent Bülow for his sixtieth birthday on 8 January 1890 a portrait of Beethoven (copper etching by Michalek) with a "cordial greeting from Vienna" (BBS VIII [7], p. 289, footnote 3) along with the original handwritten score of Symphony no. 3, op. 90. Brahms's dedication on the title page read, "For dearly loved Hans von Bülow / in loyal friendship. / Johs Brahms," dated "Vienna, 8 January 1890." As further inventories show, this exemplar remained the property of Marie von Bülow until 1911; today it

is held by the Library of Congress in Washington, D.C. In an accompanying letter, Brahms wrote,

> *I completely agree with the previous speaker, who just told you and wished you the most beautiful and splendid things! On my part be greeted by what I take to be a fine new portrait of Beethoven. I have to say that it is not the brave engraver's fault that I didn't add a picture of myself! Today I'm almost sorry that I stubbornly refused him.*
>
> *On days like today one desires to be as personal as possible! Let me come, then, to the second part of my package—the part that doesn't resemble me! I happen to still have the autograph score for my Symphony in F major. Sending it to you almost gives me the feeling that I'm shaking your hand. That's all it means, and now I shall make room for the next speaker.*
>
> *Hear him in good humor and think of the friends you love, they are with you in their thoughts, and of course, let the most beautiful choir sing for you! With all my heart, Your J. Brahms.* (Kalbeck 4/1, p. 185, footnote 1)

6. Bülow used the same stationery (containing the printed statement) as mentioned in letter no. 40.

Letter No. 45

Sign. : Mus. ep. Hans von Bülow 323. One double page, written on three sides (1r, 2r, postscript on 1v [lengthwise]).

1. It is not clear which articles are meant. For more on the context of Brahms's inquiry, see letter no. 46, note 2.

2. Eduard Hanslick. The topic of this paragraph is unclear. The *Neue Freie Presse* contains no feuilleton articles by Hanslick in the months preceding this letter that would explain these lines. "Goldmann" is the name Bülow uses for Chrysander (see subsequent letters).

3. Violinist Max Brode (1850–1917) gave up his virtuoso career in 1876 due to finger trouble. He became concertmaster in Königsberg, where he launched a series of symphony concerts. Bülow was a guest conductor and soloist at one of them on 16 January 1890.

4. Cellist Heberlin (first name unknown, born in 1861) performed in Königsberg as a member of Brode's trio; in the 1890s he immigrated to the United States.

5. A return visit to Königsberg to conduct the Double Concerto op. 120 never happened.

6. See letter no. 43, note 3.

7. Brahms became acquainted with singer Hermine Spies (1857–1893) during the summer of 1883, when she sang the solo part of his Alto Rhap-

sody op. 53. Brahms was very impressed. On Therese Simon, see letter no. 44, note 4.

8. Gustav Dömpke (1853–1923), in the 1870s a critic for the Königsberg General News (*Königsberger Allgemeine Zeitung*); from 1883 to 1887 he was a music critic, as successor to Max Kalbeck, at the *Vienna General News* (*Wiener Allgemeine Zeitung*). He then returned to Königsberg and wrote reviews.

9. Singer Julius Stockhausen (1826–1906) became close friends with Brahms in 1856. In 1878/79 he was a singing instructor at the Hoch Conservatory; afterward he directed his own school for song in Frankfurt until his death. Stockhausen's intention to return to the Hoch Conservatory after Raff's death, from whom he had estranged himself after a disagreement, was the immediate reason for splitting the Raff Conservatory, where Bülow gave summer courses from 1884 to 1887 (see letter no. 20, note 1). Spengel's fear that Stockhausen's move to Hamburg would create competition for his Cäcilien Association proved to be unfounded.

Letter No. 46

Sign.: Mus. ep. Hans von Bülow 324. One double page, written on two sides (1r, 2r).

1. Brahms's suggestion (see note 2 below) concerns a gift that a group of unnamed Hamburg patrons gave Bülow for his sixtieth birthday on 8 January 1890. The main passage of the document, designed in great detail by Hamburg's landscape painter Ascan Lutteroth (1842–1923), reads,

> After careful consideration we have reached the conclusion that no one better than you yourself knows the most appropriate way to make a worthy contribution to the beloved art. Thus we allow ourselves to present you with a little material token of our idealistic enthusiasm and request that you use this sum of ten thousand marks as you see fit for an artistic purpose that your great expertise acknowledges as being the most worthy. (SBB, Sign.: Mus. NL Hans von Bülow F II, 2)

2. Once the gift from the Hamburg patrons had become public, Brahms wrote to Bülow asking (after first discussing at length Hamburg's music author Josef Sittard),

> *What will you do with the 10,000 marks? Not spend it, I hope, on stipends for piano houris [lovely maidens]? I have often thought that when the Handel edition is completed, it would be decent to give Chrysander some compensation. But I'm not the person to organize such things and I shy from the publicity, even in a case such as this.* (BBS VIII [7], p. 290, footnote 1. See also a more detailed quotation of the letter in Geiringer, p. 187.)

Outstanding music historian Friedrich Chrysander (1826–1901), editor of the *Denkmäler der Tonkunst* [Monuments of the Art of Music] (published from 1869 to 1871) and publisher of the *Vierteljahrsschrift für Musikwissenschaft* [Musicology Quarterly] (1885 ff., founded jointly with Philipp Spitta and Guido Adler), lived as of 1866 as a private scholar in Hamburg. His lifework was the complete edition of the works of Handel and a (unfinished) Handel biography.

3. Eduard Hanslick.

4. Chrysander.

5. Joseph Joachim.

6. Heinrich von Herzogenberg; the reference is to String Quartet op. 63 (published in Leipzig by Rieter-Biedermann in 1890), performed by the Joachim Quartet on 28 January 1890.

7. Beethoven's String Quartet op. 127.

8. The first item on the program of the "8th Hamburg Subscription Concert" on 5 February 1890 was the Serenade in D major op. 11.

Letter No. 47

Sign.: Mus. ep. Hans von Bülow 325. One double page, written on three sides (1r, 2r, postscript on 1v [lengthwise]).

1. Vincenzo Bellini (1801–1835), *Norma* (premiére on 26 December 1831); W. A. Mozart (1756–1791), *Le nozze di Figaro* (premiére on 1 May 1786).

2. The famous portrait showing Brahms and Bülow (1889) made at the Brasch photography studio in Berlin.

3. Chrysander's place of residence.

4. Bülow more or less cites the fourth verse from Lorenzo de' Medici's (1449–1492) "Canzona di Bacco": "*Quant'è bella giovinezza, / che si fugge tuttavia! / Chi vuol esser lieto, sia: / di doman non c'è certezza.*"

5. Eduard Hanslick.

Letter No. 48

Sign.: Mus. ep. Hans von Bülow 326. One double page, written on four sides (1r, 2r, 1v [lengthwise], 2v [lengthwise]).

1. Although Bülow writes "recent," the quotation in question is apparently the Brahms line that Bülow used in his article on enharmonics (see letter no. 42, note 3). In an undated (perhaps January?) letter that seems to have been a reply to Bülow's letter no. 43, Brahms wrote that Bülow's quotation of Brahms's words on the perfection of Mozart's ideal composing "*can't be correct: I probably said 'since we really cannot compose as perfectly' or, more likely, 'since*

we can compose neither as perfectly nor as beautifully,' etc." (BBS VIII [7], p. 312, footnote 1).

Except for this Brahms letter of uncertain dating, their correspondence appears to have stagnated between Bülow's letters no. 47 and 48, which might explain why Bülow, despite the long interval, nevertheless writes "recent."

2. The last item on the program of the first subscription concert (Hamburg, 20 October 1890) was Symphony no. 1, op 68, conducted by Bülow.

3. In the nineteenth century, critics and ardent followers alike considered Vincenzo Bellini's (1801–1835) opera music the epitome of bel canto.

4. Wilhelm Tieftrunk (1846–1930) was a member of the orchestra and first flutist for the "new subscription concerts" beginning with season 1890/91. On renegades from Julius Bernuth's orchestra, see letter no. 35, note 8.

5. Johannes Brahms, Symphony no. 1, op. 68, fourth movement, measure 38 ff.

Letter No. 49

Sign.: Mus. ep. Hans von Bülow 328. One double page, written on three sides (1r, 2r, postscript on 1v [lengthwise], stationery with black mourning border (as on letter no. 21).

1. Marcus Tullius Cicero (106–43 BC), De officiis 1:5: "Suum cuique"— "Viribus unitis" was the motto chosen by Emporer Franz Joseph I by "divine providence" on 12 February 1848. In younger years, Bülow liked to apply the slogan ironically to concerts that he (as successor to his teacher Liszt) gave as a sole performer, which was by no means customary at the time (BBS IV [3], p. 285).

Bülow's letter to Chrysander can be found in BBS VIII (7), p. 21f. The passage mentioning Brahms reads,

> In an effort to make the best decision, I asked our joint friend, illustrious composer Dr. Johannes Brahms for advice, which he, reflecting his role as an honorary citizen of Hamburg, kindly gave.
>
> The result is the deep conviction that for this donation no better purpose can be found than to put it at the disposal of the principal representative of German musicology . . . , alias *Doctor Friedrich Chrysander* to use at will for the continuation of his work of cultural-historical and practical interest for the benefit of this and future generations.

2. Bülow considered pianist and composer Eugen d'Albert (1864–1932) the best pianist of the younger generation. D'Albert's acquaintance with Brahms (arranged through his teacher Hans Richter) dates from 6 February 1882, following a Brahms soirée given by Bülow. The strain of that evening,

however, cost Bülow interest in any immediate new acquaintance, and thus he did not personally meet D'Albert until 1884 when the latter gave a concert in Dresden on 10 March, to which Bülow reacted enthusiastically.

3. At the turn of the year 1890/91, Brahms had a case of the flu (cf. Kalbeck 4/1, p. 226f.).

4. Composer Theodor Kirchner (1823–1903) was trained in music in part at the Leipzig Conservatory. As of 1843 he was an organist at Winterthur, and from 1862 to 1875 he was a conductor and music instructor in Zurich. His friendship with Brahms dates from the year 1856. After working in various cities in Germany (eventually at the conservatory in Dresden), Kirchner lived as of 1890 in Hamburg without a job and under great financial hardship.

5. During the season in Hamburg, the following concerts conducted by Bülow included works by Robert Schumann: the third subscription concert, on 17 November 1890 (Symphony no. 1, op. 38); the fifth subscription concert, on 15 December 1890 ("Genoveva" Overture); and the sixth subscription concert, on 5 January 1891 (Symphony no. 3, op. 97).

6. Possibly encouraged by one of Bülow's reports, Antonie (Toni) Petersen (1840–1909), daughter of the mayor of Hamburg, had asked Brahms for the yet unpublished score of String Quintet op. 111. As we know from Brahms's reply to Toni Petersen dated 2 February 1891, he had already sent it to his publisher Simrock (Kurt Hofmann, "Brahmsiana der Familie Petersen," in *Brahms-Studien* 3 [Hamburg, 1979], p. 94).

7. Joseph Joachim had the quintet performed from the handwritten score on 10 February 1890 in Berlin.

Letter No. 50

Sign.: Mus. ep. Hans von Bülow 329. One double page, written on three sides (1r+v, 2r), black mourning border (like letters no. 21 and 49).

1. Brahms reacted to this inquiry as follows:

Dear Friend!

When one has done something good and right, or believes to have done so, one may calmly await the outcome. This is the situation you find yourself in momentarily and you should ban useless thoughts and fantasies (about someone finding your deed worthless, etc.). Chrysander is a quaint soul and you can neither know nor intuit what is now going through his mind. Whether he is for or against accepting your gift, he can only think the very best of you and your offer. I see myself in both your shoes and his and can learn something from both of you. If I were Chrysander, I would have learned [by all of this] that in cases such as these one should immediately say something provisional. But if I were you, I too would tend much too much to walk through the gloomiest minor key! And finally, I must say that I am pleased to think that Chrysander might—touched and cheerily grateful—refuse [your offer] *because he absolutely needs no more money. . . . Dear Friend, I'm startled by my own chatter. . . . But I believe that the first sentence of this letter says it all. If you don't share this belief and have still not heard anything from Chrysander, then send me a note and I'll write to him. I can do that all the more graciously because I can, as I said, see myself acting as he did. . . . Now, be patient, and accept my greetings.*

Wholly your J. Brahms

(Geiringer, p. 188)

2. Eduard Hanslick's concert critique in the *Neue Freie Presse* from 6 January 1891 discussing Edvard Grieg's (1843–1907) first *Peer Gynt* suite, that he felt "contains more poetry and appreciation of art than Ibsen's entire five-act monster." Eduard Hanslick, *Aus dem Tagebuche eines Musikers* [From the Diary of a Musician], *Modern Opera*, part 6 (Berlin [3] 1892), p. 335. Bülow's malicious characterization of Grieg alludes to the latter's friendship with Max Abraham, director of Leipzig's publishing house Peters.

3. Bülow's initial enthusiasm for Ibsen cooled off permanently after becoming familiar with the drama *Hedda Gabler*.

4. Adolf von Wilbrandt (1837–1911) was director of Vienna's Burgtheater from 1881 to 1887 and also wrote novels and tragedies.

Ernst von Wildenbruch (1845–1909) was not only a successful author, but also a brilliant diplomat (1877, Ministry of Foreign Affairs in Berlin; 1897, privy legation councilor).

5. The oratorio "Konstantin" by Georg Vierling (1820–1901) that Bülow heard in the Berlin Philharmonic on 9 January 1891, performed by the Stern Singing Society.

6. "Burlesque" for piano and orchestra (1885) by Richard Strauss, conducted by Bülow in Berlin on 12 January 1891 at the sixth philharmonic concert; the soloist was Eugen d'Albert.

7. The Academic Festival Overture closed the program of the concert mentioned in note 6 above.

Letter No. 51

Sign.: Mus. ep. Hans von Bülow 330. One double page, written on two sides (1r, 2r), black mourning border (as in letters no. 21, 41, and 50).

1. [A German adage: *Abwarten und Tee trinken.*]

2. Violinist Marie Soldat (1863–1955), who after her marriage in 1889 went by the name Soldat-Roeger, had through Brahms become a pupil of Joseph Joachim and was the first female interpreter of Brahms's Violin Concerto.

Bülow's question refers to a mistaken indication of her year of birth based on the inversion of the last two digits of the already erroneous year of 1864 indicated in Schuberth's conversation lexicon of music: "Soldat, Marie, born in Graz on 25 March 1846." Emil Breslauer, ed., *Julius Schuberth's Musikalisches Conversations-Lexikon*, 11th ed. (Leipzig, no year of publication [it was 1891]).

Letter No. 52

   Sign.: Mus. ep. Hans von Bülow 331. One double page, written on three sides (1r, 2r, 1v [lengthwise], black mourning border (as in letters no. 21, 49, 50, and 51).
   1. In a review (dated 16 January 1891) for the second Society Concert from 11 January 1891, which began with J. S. Bach's cantata "Ich hatte viel Beküm-mernis" (BVW 21), Eduard Hanslick objected to the aesthetics of the soprano ("soul") and basso ("Jesus") duet, mentioning that when he had once before brought forward the same objection, "a major leaseholder on the Bach cult" (meaning Philipp Spitta) had given him a good scolding. In this concert review, then, Hanslick mentions with satisfaction that meanwhile Spitta's classic Bach monograph itself calls the duet in question "a sore spot" in the cantata, adding the following fundamental remark to which, in particular, Bülow's reaction refers: "I believe that both famous musicologists, Spitta and Chrysander, would have cultivated and strengthened much more genuine love for Bach and Handel had they now and again, as in the present case, really said 'what unfortunately must be said'" (*Neue Freie Presse*, no. 9480, 16 January 1891, p. 1).
   2. By ironically labeling it a "correspondence card," Bülow refers to a letter from Chrysander to Bülow, dated 15 January 1891, containing a long report on Chrysander's research work but not mentioning Bülow's monetary offer at all. Chrysander's original letter, which Bülow enclosed in this letter to Brahms, has not survived, but a fourteen-page copy exists. The passage that Bülow marked for Brahms's attention, where Chrysander reflects on why even trained musicians dislike Bach and Handel, reads as follows:

> At this point I would like to simply appeal to the judgment of the most noble and unprejudiced artist, to whom I have the honor of writing these lines, and ask you whether you, in Handel's case, have not found among the greatest, even unsurpassable things, also bits that are less acceptable, sometimes even disagreeable, a bare cadence, a stenciled formation, overly uniform parts, a harsh cantilena, or one made monotonous by repetition, a dry recitative, lacking individuality or exclaimed carelessly, too much simi-larity among roulades, sometimes even a paltry harmony, and so on. (SBB, Sign.: Mus. ep. F. Chrysander 2001 [copy], pp. 5/6)

Chrysander excuses these deficiencies by noting that Handel composed too swiftly, "at a speed unknown to any other composer" (SBB, Sign.: Mus. ep. F. Chrysander 2001 [copy], pp. 516).

Bülow asked Brahms to pass Chrysander's letter on to Hanslick, who replied at length (to Bülow) in a letter dated 23 January 1891. Hanslick's reaction to the passage marked by Bülow (the entire letter can be found in BBS VIII [7], p. 328f.) reads,

> The prosaic inquiry that you marked in blue, namely, whether in Handel['s works] you have not perhaps occasionally discovered "less acceptable bits," bare cadences, monotonous roulades, etc., made me laugh. As if there were any question about it! If you ask me, Spitta's idolatry, and even more so that of Chrysander, who always seems like [grand inquisitor] Peter Arbuez or an irritable old maid to me, has had no beneficial consequences. Some of his readers become hypocrites, others tire of his eternal scolding and want to drop the whole thing. *Prior* to reading Chrysander's book, Handel's roulades simply bored me; now that I am always reminded that Chrysander commands us to see them as miraculous marks of character, full of dramatic force and musical beauty, I find them annoying.

3. As part of Chrysander's project *Monuments of Composition*, Brahms had edited the first and second book of piano pieces by Françoise Couperin (1668–1733). *Denkmäler der Tonkunst* 4 (Bergedorf, 1871).

Besides Handel and Couperin, the other composers Bülow mentions here are Arcangelo Corelli (1653–1713) and Giacomo Carissimi (1605–1674).

4. French historian André Duchesne (1584–1640) is considered the father of French history. *Nouvelle biographie générale*, vol. 14 (Copenhagen, 1965), p. 947.

5. For "Goldmann" (nickname for Chrysander), see letter no. 46, note 4. Bülow's estate contains a reprint from the January issue of the *Vierteljahrsschrift für Musikwissenschaft* [Quarterly for Musicology] 7 (1892): pp. 1–25. Friedrich Chrysander, "Eine Klavier-Phantasie von Karl Philipp Emanuel Bach mit nachträglich von Gerstenberg eingefügten Gesangsmelodien zu zwei verschieden Texten" [A fantasy for the piano by K. Ph. Em. Bach, including song melodies added later by Gerstenberg for two different texts] (SBB, Sign.: Db 323). It was perhaps this separate reprint that Bülow asked Brahms to return.

Letter No. 53

Sign.: Mus. ep. Hans von Bülow 332. One double page, written on four sides (1r+v, 2r+v).

*Wilhelmshatz, perhaps a play on the name of the city Wilhelmshaven.

1. See letter no. 54 for the correct form and source of this quotation.

2. Hanslick's letter dated 23 January 1891 (cf. letter no. 52, note 2). For Bülow's herewith announced reply to Hanslick (from Hamburg, dated 29 January 1891), see BBS VIII (7), pp. 329–331.

3. In the closing scene of Goethe's *Faust: Der Tragödie zweiter Teil* (part 2 of the Tragedy of Faust), Gretchen appears in the role of *una poenitentium* (the sole penitent).

4. The third item on the program for the "7th Philharmonic Concert" (Berlin, 26 January 1891) was the première, from the manuscript score and under Bülow's conducting, of the *Ouvertüre zu Shakespeares Heinrich IV* (Overture to Shakespeare's Henry IV), composed in 1854 by Joseph Joachim (cf. also BBW VI, p. 261: Joachim sought to know from Brahms whether, as Bülow had claimed, the première of Joachim's early work fulfilled a long-held wish). The score to this piece was never published; in 1856 Brahms worked out an arrangement for two pianos that was published in 1902.

5. Heinrich Schliemann (1822–1890), German archeologist, discoverer and excavator of the ancient Greek ruins of Troy (1870–1882) and Mycenae (1874–1876).

6. Beethoven's String Quartet op. 59, 1.

7. The clippings have not survived. The sixth Hamburg subscription concert on 19 January 1891 closed with the enthusiastically received Symphony no. 3.

8. After Bülow had resigned from his obligations in Bremen at the end of the 1888/89 season, Max Erdmannsdörfer (1848–1905) took over the subscriptions concerts, thereafter called "philharmonic concerts" (from 1889 to 1895). From 1871 to 1880 Erdmannsdörfer had been the royal conductor in Sondershausen and successfully revived the "Loh Concerts" that propagated Liszt's orchestral works under the direction of Eduard Stein (1818–1864). Bülow's disfavor with Erdmannsdörfer goes back to the first experience they had of working together. In June 1878 at the fifteenth convention of musicians organized by the ADMV in Erfurt, Bülow was to play the Piano Concerto in F-sharp minor by Hans von Bronsart under the direction of Erdmannsdörfer. The rehearsal was so unsatisfactory [lacking a trace of edification] that Liszt took over conducting the orchestra (see Lina Ramann's depiction of the "quarrels" between Bülow and Erdmannsdörfer, in *Lisztiana* [Kassel, 1983], p. 128).

Letter No. 54

Sign.: Mus. ep. Hans von Bülow 333. One double page, written on four sides (1r+v, 2r+v), black mourning border (as in letters no. 21, 49, 50, 51, and 52). Enclosure: Printed program.

1. Cellist David Popper (1843–1913) was concertmaster at the Vienna Court Opera from 1868 to 1873 and thereafter a virtuoso without steady employment. On 16 February 1891 he played the solo part at the ninth subscrip-

tion concert in Hamburg. Bülow had been enthusiastic about Popper when the latter was young (cf. BBS IV [3], p. 573; letter to Joachim Raff dated 30 January 1864). See 2 Samuel 19:9–10 for what it means to "act like Saul."

2. Joseph Hellmesberger (1828–1893), famous violin virtuoso and first violin of a string quartet. As of 1851 he was director of the Society of the Friends of Music and as of 1859 director of the Vienna Conservatory.

3. Alice Barbi (1862–1948). Next to Amalie Joachim and Hermine Spies she became the third important interpreter of Brahms lieder. Brahms met her on 5 April 1892. After marrying Baron Wolf-Stromersee she resigned from concert appearances in December 1893; at her farewell concert in Vienna on 21 December 1893 Brahms accompanied her at the piano.

4. Hermine Spies (cf. letter no. 45, note 7).

5. See letter no. 53, note 1. "Wen reut, was er getan, fehlt zweimal: Weil er's getan, und dann, weil's ihn gereut."

6. See letter no. 53, note 2.

7. On 20 February 1891, Chrysander's revised notice appeared in the Hamburg News (*Hamburger Nachrichten*) (which due to its political bent Bülow nicknamed after Bismarck's old-age residence Friedrichsruhe). The announcement first informs of how the donated sum will be used: 2,500 marks "to produce a photo-lithographical facsimile of the original manuscript of *Messiah* by Handel . . . , this marvel of music that the master composed from the first to the last note in just twenty-three days," and 7,500 marks to procure historical instruments for Hamburg's Museum of Art and Craft. The closing paragraph reads,

> Thus, thanks to the providence of both Gentlemen and Donors of this gift the interests have been met of both the entire world of music and Hamburg's Art Collections in a manner true and fruitful for all future times: The production of a facsimile of the original manuscript of Handel's *Messiah*: this beloved masterpiece of the most noble German art is of lasting value for the piety of posterity. By founding a collection of good historical musical instruments Hamburg is assured a museum had presently only by a few outstanding centers of music, making a praiseworthy epoch from the history of the development of Hamburg's craftwork known to [citizens of] today.

8. The apparatus used in electrotherapy for Bülow's chronic headaches was named after the inventor of modern electrotherapy, Guillaume Benjamin Armand Duchenne (1806–1875), whose last name was sometimes written to include his place of birth: Duchenne de Boulogne.

9. Allusion to the name of a collection by Carl Reinecke that was reprinted several times (on Carl Reinecke see letter no. 32, note 13): *Unsere Lieblinge: Die schönsten Melodien alter und neuer Zeit in leichter Bearbeitung für das*

Pianoforte [Our Favorites: The most beautiful melodies from past and modern times in easy arrangements for the piano], first published in Leipzig in 1869 consisting of four booklets.

10. Wilhelm Kienzl (1857–1941) from Graz was hired as conductor for Hamburg's City Theater in January 1891. As early as 13 February 1891 and with reference to an anonymous source in Hamburg, the *Allgemeine Deutsche Musik-Zeitung* (vol. 18, no. 7 [1891]) reported that Kienzl had been fired. Among other things, the paper wrote that the performance of Cherubini's *Le porteur d'eau* [The Water Carrier] exhibited "very alarming deviations" (p. 90). Two weeks later the *ADMZ* (vol. 18, no. 9 [1891]) printed a counterstatement by Kienzl in which he, "in the interest of my artistic reputation," refused to accept the *ADMZ*'s anonymous report on how he had conducted *The Water Carrier*, citing also two very positive reviews from Hamburg (p. 120).

The Water Carrier (*Les deux journées ou Le porteur d'eau*) by Luigi Cherubini (1760–1842) had its première on 16 January 1800 in Paris and was part of the Hamburg City Theater's repertory as of 1855. After 27 January 1888 its new production was performed as directed by Hans von Bülow.

11. Bülow alludes here to events surrounding the succession of Carl Müller (1818–1894) as conductor of the Frankfurt Museum Concerts, a position for which over fifty persons applied. With sixty-one to five votes, the choice was made on 12 February 1891 for Bülow's protégé Gustav Kogel (1849–1921), director of the Berlin Philharmonic's popular concerts. The contract was limited to three years. The Museum Society's members who were entitled to vote were not informed by the board of the names of the applicants until two days prior to the general assembly. Due to this scandalous procedure, long-standing members of the board Theodor Mettenheimer and Heinrich Hanau resigned one night before the general meeting. In line with the nature of this policy of secrecy, it has not been possible to find clues as to the complete list of applicants either in Frankfurt's local newspapers or in musical publications. The museum's files were destroyed in World War II. The names of a few applicants have become known: Wilhelm Kienzl, Ludwig Rottenberg, Felix Weingartner, Hermann Kretzschmar, Gustav Mahler, and Rafael Maszkowski, whom Brahms had recommended, but who withdrew his application. Thus we do not know whom Bülow means by "little Fritz from Rotterdam," someone who competed with his favorite candidate, Kogel, but lost. It is possibly Friedrich Gernsheim (1839–1916), who belonged to both Bülow's and Brahms's circle of friends and who moved in 1890 back to Berlin from Rotterdam, where he had worked since 1874.

On Bülow's involvement in this episode see a letter he wrote to his daughter Daniela on 17 February 1891: "You might suspect that behind the scenes I had a not insignificant part in affairs regarding the conductor for

Frankfurt's concerts" (*Neue Briefe,* p. 697f.). Of course, Bülow only favored Kogel for lack of a more suitable candidate: "The restricting of his contract to three years was my doing, after first eliminating even worst applicants" (*Neue Briefe,* p. 699). Despite the time limit (which ended after Bülow's death), Kogel remained conductor of the museum's concerts until 1903.

12. "Seven Folksongs by August Bungert, arranged for piano by Theodor Kirchner, op. 49," published by Luckhardt in Berlin, pub. nos. 839–845. These are nos. 2, 3, 7, 13, 20, and 28 from Lieder Collection op. 49 by Bungert (1845–1915).

Letter No. 55

Sign.: Mus. ep. Hans von Bülow 334. One double page, written on three sides (1r+v, 2r).

1. Bismarck (to whom Bülow is alluding here) and Moltke were also honorary citizens of Hamburg. Marie von Bülow reports on said dinner:

> On 16 January of this year [1892], Mayor Petersen invited the Bismarck family to a festive dinner, to which we were also invited. The impression left by this experience and its effect were elementary. When a toast was made to the well-being of the baronial couple, Bülow rose and shouted ebulliently "When the Jews saw God, they ate and drank. (Marie von Bülow, *Hans von Bülow in Leben und Wort* [Stuttgart, 1925], p. 178)

2. Rafael Maszkowski (1838–1901). As of 1890 he was the conductor of Breslau's Orchestra Association. After Bülow left the Berlin Philharmonic Orchestra, Maszkowski was one of several interim conductors (including Hans Richter, Felix Mottl, Hermann Levi, and others).

3. Allusion to the dates of the French Revolution: outbreak of the revolution in 1789 and rule of the Committee of Public Safety under Danton and Robespierre in 1793.

4. Theodor Kirchner. Bülow's efforts for Kirchner, who after having settled in Hamburg in 1890 experienced great financial hardship, culminated shortly after this letter in participating in one of Kirchner's concerts in Hamburg (3 March 1892, "Concert by Theodor Kirchner with kind cooperation by Dr. Hans von Bülow" and others; Bülow's name was printed larger than the others), where Bülow performed Schumann's *Faschingsschwank aus Wien* [Carnival Story from Vienna], op. 26. On the printed program found among Bülow's papers, Bülow had written in pencil, "Kirchner played 2 piano pieces as an encore" (SBB, Sign.: Db 1815 [6]).

5. Bülow originally wrote that he barked "at him," but crossed it out and wrote "at her."

6. Marie von Bülow wrote on the page in pencil, "In reality his reply was better. He said 'anyone that's fluid [has cash] is not superfluous.'"

7. Changed from "he" to "she."

8. Paraphrased wording from Max Kalbeck's German text arrangement for Mozart's *Don Giovanni*, alluding to Leporello's reaction to movements the statue makes in the cemetery scene (act 2, scene 11): "Woe, his head nods, his head nods! What does it mean?" (W. A. Mozart, *Don Juan*, piano arrangement by Johann Nepomuk Fuchs, "An arrangement for the German stage based on the Italian original by Max Kalbeck" [Vienna: Albert J. Gutmann, 1887, pub. no. A.J.G. 650], p. 250f.) The exemplar of the piano arrangement that Bülow used for his production of *Don Juan* at Hamburg's City Theater (première on 29 Oct. 1887) can be found among Bülow's remaining papers (SBB, Sign.: Km 579/5).

9. Julius Spengel's son.

10. Here Bülow cites the identical programs of the closing concerts in Hamburg and Berlin, which in a demonstrative gesture display the musico-historical triad—Bach, Beethoven, and Brahms—often evoked by Bülow. The concert in Berlin on 28 March simultaneously marked the—preliminary—end of Bülow's cooperation with the Philharmonic Orchestra.

Letter No. 56

Sign.: Mus. ep. Hans von Bülow 335. One double page, written on two sides (1r+v), black mourning border (paper format identical to letters no. 21, 49, 50, 51, and 52).

1. Victor von Bojanowski, as of 1862 married to Bülow's sister Isidore. He had been imperial general consul in London, but resigned from the position for health reasons. Bismarck's public praise for Bojanowski (cf. BBS VIII [7], p. 235, footnote 1) contributed considerably to Bülow's pride in his brother-in-law.

2. At the end of his last concert in Berlin (tenth philharmonic concert, 28 March 1892), which closed with Beethoven's *Eroica*, Bülow addressed the audience and symbolically dedicated the *Eroica* to ex-chancellor Bismarck, who had recently been dismissed. The response from Berlin's audience and press was hostile. At a concert in Hamburg set for the date of Bismarck's birthday (1 April 1882), Bülow repeated and strengthened his rededication of the *Eroica* by supplementing the printed program with a self-written hymn on Bismarck as a text for the finale theme. In contrast to the reaction in Berlin, the response in Hamburg was thoroughly positive. When Bülow returned to Berlin on 4

April, where he had to finish off some concert obligations (4, 5, and 6 April), he was surprised that the public and press celebrated him enthusiastically.

3. Johann Wolfgang von Goethe, *Faust: The Tragedy, Part Two*, verse 11,511. Mephistopheles calls out, "*Herbei, herbei! Herein, herein! Ihr schlotternden Lemuren. Aus Bändern, Sehnen und Gebein, geflickte Halbnaturen.*" "Come on, come on! Come in, come in! You wobbly lemures, you tendinous, sinewy, bony half-creatures." [Lemures: the spirits of the dead in ancient Rome.]

4. Bülow had put Brahms's Serenade in A major op. 16 on three programs: 21 March 1892 (Hamburg, tenth subscription concert), 28 March 1892 (Berlin, tenth philharmonic concert), and 5 April 1892 (a philharmonic concert in Berlin that took place after the season was over). Here he probably also exuberantly counted the three dress rehearsals that were open to the public.

5. Simrock.

6. At the celebration for Bismarck (1 April 1892), Bülow had met Bismarck's longtime friend, painter Franz Lenbach (1836–1904). Lenbach immediately suggested painting Bülow's portrait, and in April Bülow went to Munich to sit for some sketches.

7. The birthday present, Berlioz's score for *Damnation de Faust*, is listed in Brahms's index of music items: "Faust. Score (Paris, Richault), French and German text" (Hofmann, p. 149).

8. In April 1892 Brahms replied:

I'm just in time, while you're happily packing your bags, to wish you the nicest and cheeriest things for the trip. Incidentally, I see it as the best sign of the best health that you are traveling to Italy instead of giving piano instruction in Frankfurt, you will breathe the wonderful air and bathe in beauty. . . . Why don't I come along, every trip I've taken there was lovelier and more valuable than the last . . . . Are you headed for Palermo? My greetings can accompany you at least that far! Why then is my usual, dear companion in Italy [Widmann from Bern] *staying home this time? Because it doesn't take just the right attitude, you have to have the same spry legs, too.* (Geiringer, p. 197f.)

Letter No. 57

Sign.: Mus. ep. Hans von Bülow 336. One double page, written on four sides (1r+v, 2r+v).

1. Hermann Wolff's new concert hall in Berlin, the Bechstein Hall, was to be ceremoniously opened for use on the fourth, fifth, and sixth of October 1892 by three concerts (on the fourth with a piano performance by Bülow; on the fifth with Joachim's string quartet in cooperation with Brahms and Richard Mühlfeld; and on the sixth by Anton Rubinstein). Compositions by

Brahms, among other pieces, had been announced for Bülow's performance. In this regard, Brahms wrote to Bülow from Ischl in late July,

> *Dear Friend,*
>
> *Unfortunately, of all of your composers for October 4, I am the only one who can still write music. So the best compliment we can make together is that I ask you: Wouldn't you like to play a new little piece in the new hall?*
>
> *You might prefer to take it easy and enjoy your September in peace. But if you are tempted, do send a word to Ischl and I'll send you a trial booklet for "inspection and selection."*
>
> *With cordial greetings, your*
J. Brahms

(BBS VIII [7], p. 395f.)

These were the compositions written during Brahms's summer stay in Ischl, Seven Fantasies for Piano, op. 116.

2. *Beard*, German: *Bart*. An allusion to Karl Heinrich Barth (1847–1922). As of 1871 Barth was professor for piano at Berlin's college of music. During a summer visit in Ischl he had already seen the new compositions, and it was through him that Bülow already knew about them.

3. Brahms's response to this request (postmark: Ischl, 8 Aug. 1892):

> *Now, you too, Brutus!*
>
> *I take you by your dagger words: You will surely agree that the best thing to do with "valses oubliées" is to really forget them.*
>
> *I have always hoped and believed that nothing could mislead me to do something like that. This summer I've had to resist half-a-dozen exhibition and master albums, and so often for more serious, worthier occasions; and now you, too, Brutus!*
>
> *Like everyone else, you have a certain intention, but all that interests me is what it means for music and the musician—and that can be many different things, as you know and consider when some other interest doesn't hinder you. It's not your poet that I think of as misleading me, it is to you and your wish that I can only respond with a sigh. Of the poet I must openly admit that he's at the very back of my bookshelf and I rarely take him out for the pleasure of it.*
>
> *The piano compositions were so startled that they fell under the table. Now that there's no hurry, I'll leave them there. With a deep sigh and greetings, your J. B.*

(BBS VIII [7], p. 398)

Despite the closing lines, Brahms did send Bülow the piano compositions. Bülow simply confirmed their receipt by a no-longer-extant telegram (see the introduction to this book). In the end, Bülow included neither the previously announced nor the new Brahms compositions in the program for 4 October. Instead, it read, Mozart's Fantasy in C major; Beethoven's Sonata op. 81a (Les Adieux); Kiel's Variations and Fugue in F minor op. 17; Schumann's *Fasch-*

ingsschwank aus Wien op. 26; Chopin's Nocturne op. 37, no. 2; Impromptu op. 36; Scherzo op. 39; and Berceuse op. 57. On the next evening Brahms, Mühlfeld, and the Joachim quartet played Brahms compositions: Sextet op. 18, Violin Concerto op. 108 (dedicated to Bülow), and Clarinet Quintet op. 115. On the third evening (Oct. 6), Anton Rubinstein performed mostly his own compositions. Due to his illness, Bülow was unable to attend the second and third concerts.

4. Play on the name Caprivi and the German word for critters: *Viecher*. The persons meant are the followers of Bismarck's successor, Georg Leo Graf von Caprivi (1831–1899, German reich chancellor from 1890 to 1894).

5. Brahms replied to Bülow's last letter with the letter cited in note 3. The very last document of written correspondence between Bülow and Brahms is a letter that Brahms sent Bülow following the special concerts on 4, 5, and 6 October 1892. Bülow was critically ill and only able to perform his piano concert with the utmost effort; afterward he had to lie down immediately and was unable to receive Brahms. He could not attend the concerts on the following two evenings. He let his wife return the manuscript for the new piano compositions to Brahms. After returning to Vienna, Brahms wrote

Dear Friend,

recently in Berlin I quietly laid the piano pieces in my valise after thinking that I cannot send them to you again because I don't know whether you like them.

Today I picked them up again and noticed, astonished and touched, that they include a copy made by your own hand! I wish I had noticed that in Berlin! My doubts would have vanished in the nicest way. I would have kept the copy you made and brought back to you the original that I wrote just for you.

If only I had seen you at all! I won't complain too much, since one of my most pleasant souvenirs was the hour I spent talking with your wife and your glorious victory on the 4th, particularly because you fought so hard for it, allows you and us to look forward with cheery confidence to the next winter campaign. If it is all right with you, I shall return the piano compositions to you via Simrock.

Best greetings to you and your wife, yours cordially,
J. Brahms

(BBS VIII [7], p. 404)

Bibliography

LETTERS AND SOURCES

Bülow's Correspondence = Hans von Bülow. *Briefe und Schriften.* Edited by Marie von Bülow. 8 volumes. Leipzig, 1895–1908.

Bülow's Letters to Brahms = Hans von Bülow. *Die Briefe an Johannes Brahms.* Edited by Hans-Joachim Hinrichsen. Tutzing, 1994.

Bülow's Letters to Richard Strauss = Hans von Bülow and Richard Strauss. *Briefwechsel.* Edited by Willi Schuh and Franz Trenner. In *Richard-Strauss-Jahrbuch 1954*, pp. 7–88. Bonn, 1953.

Bülow's New Letters = Hans von Bülow. *Neue Briefe.* Edited by Richard Graf Du Moulin Eckart. Munich, 1927.

Bülow's Writings (a selection) = Hans von Bülow. *Ausgewählte Schriften, 1850–1892.* Edited by Marie von Bülow. 2 volumes. Leipzig, 1911.

Correspondence between Franz Liszt and Hans von Bülow. Edited by La Mara [= Marie Lipsius]. Leipzig, 1898.

Cosima Wagner's Diaries = Cosima Wagner. *Die Tagebücher.* Edited by Martin Gregor-Dellin and Dietrich Mack. Munich and Zurich, 1976.

Johannes Brahms's Correspondence. Edited by the Deutsche Brahms Gesellschaft. Berlin, 1906ff. Beginning with vol. XVII, *Johannes Brahms Briefwechsel: Neue Folge.* Edited by Otto Biba and Kurt and Renate Hofmann. Tutzing, 1991ff.

MONOGRAPHS AND PAPERS

Avins, Styra. "The 'Excellent People' of the Meiningen Court Orchestra and the Third Symphony of Johannes Brahms." In *Spätphase(n)? Johannes Brahms' Werke der 1880er und 1890er Jahre: Internationales musikwissenschaftliches Symposium, Meiningen*

2008, ed. Maren Goltz, Wolfgang Sandberger, and Christiane Wiesenfeldt, pp. 32–45. Munich, 2010.

Bülow Colloquium 1994 = Herta Müller and Verona Gerasch, eds. *Beiträge zum Kolloquium: Hans von Bülow—Leben, Wirken und Vermächtnis.* Staatliche Museen Meiningen, 6–7 May 1994. Meiningen, 1995.

Erck, Alfred, Inge Erck, and Herta Müller. *Hans von Bülows Meininger Jahre.* In *Südthüringer Forschungen* 25 (1990): pp. 3–63.

Haas, Frithjof. *Hans von Bülow: Leben und Wirken; Wegbereiter für Wagner, Liszt und Brahms.* Wilhelmshaven, 2002.

Hinrichsen, Hans-Joachim. *Musikalische Interpretation: Hans von Bülow.* Beihefte zum Archiv für Musikwissenschaft 46. Stuttgart, 1999.

Hinrichsen, Hans-Joachim. "Späte Versöhnung: Die Violinsonate op. 108 und ihre Widmung an Hans von Bülow." In *Spätphase(n)? Johannes Brahms' Werke der 1880er und 1890er Jahre: Internationales musikwissenschaftliches Symposium, Meiningen 2008*, ed. Maren Goltz, Wolfgang Sandberger, and Christiane Wiesenfeldt, pp. 129–140. Munich, 2010.

Mühlfeld, Christian. *Die herzogliche Hofkapelle in Meiningen: Biographisches und Statistisches.* Meiningen, 1910.

Reimann, Heinrich. *Aus Hans von Bülows Lehrzeit: Erster Teil einer unvollendet gebliebenen Biographie des Künstlers.* Edited by Heinrich Meisner. Berlin, 1908.

Stargardt-Wolff, Edith. *Wegbereiter großer Musiker: Unter Verwendung von Tagebuchblättern, Briefen und vielen persönlichen Erinnerungen von Hermann und Louise Wolff, den Gründern der ersten Konzertdirektion 1880–1935.* Berlin and Wiesbaden, 1954.

Strauss, Richard. *Erinnerungen an Hans von Bülow.* In *Betrachtungen und Erinnerungen*, by Richard Strauss, ed. Willi Schuh, pp. 183–193. Munich, 1989. (Richard Strauss. *Recollections & Reflections.* Trans. L. J. Lawrence. London, 1953).

Vogel, Bernhard. *Hans von Bülow: Sein Leben und sein Entwickelungsgang.* Leipzig, 1887.

Walker, Alan. *Hans von Bülow: A Life and Times.* Oxford and New York, 2010.

Weissheimer, Wendelin. *Erlebnisse mit Richard Wagner, Franz Liszt und vielen anderen Zeitgenossen nebst deren Briefen.* Stuttgart and Leipzig, 1898.

Zabel, Eugen. *Hans von Bülow: Gedenkblätter aus seinen letzten Lebensjahren.* Hamburg, 1894.

Name Index

Each number indicates the number of a *letter*. Numbers in roman type indicate that the name is mentioned in the letter, and where applicable, in the commentary to that letter. Numbers in italic type indicate mention exclusively in the commentary.

Abbass, Max 8, 27
Abraham, Max 50
Adler, Guido *46*
Aeschylus 14, 41, 42
D'Albert, Eugen 49; *35, 50*
D'Albert, Louise 35
Alexander, Landgrave of Hesse 27, 32
Avé-Lallement, Theodor 35

Bach, Carl Philipp Emanuel 37, 39; *52*
Bach, Johann Sebastian 14, 52, 55
Bachrich, Sigismund 22
Barbi, Alice 54
Bargheer, Carl Louis 35
Bargiel, Woldemar 44
Barth, Karl Heinrich 57
Beckerath, Laura von 38
Beckerath, Rudolf von 32; *38*
Beethoven, Ludwig van 14, 18, 21, 24, 27, 28, 41, 46, 53, 55; *1, 3, 9, 12, 22, 23, 44*
Bellini, Vincenzo 47, 48
Berlioz, Hector 24, 56; *18, 21, 23, 35, 44*
Bernsdorf, Eduard *10*

Bernuth, Julius von 35, 48
Billroth, Theodor 37, 44; *16, 35*
Bismarck, Otto von 55, 56, 57; *54*
Bismarck, Wilhelm (Bill) von 33
Bizet, Georges *30*
Böhme (music publisher) 37, 38, 43, 57; *42*
Boieldieu, François-Adrien 37
Boito, Arrigo *33*
Bojanowski, Victor von 56
Breitkopf & Härtel (music publishers) 20
Breslauer, Emil 51
Brode, Max 45
Brodsky, Adolf 27, 28, 35
Bronsart, Hans von 1, 2; *12, 40, 53*
Bruch, Max *1*
Bruckner, Anton 22, 41, 48, 51; *20, 33*
Brüll, Ignaz 22, 35, 41
Bülow, Blandine von *12*
Bülow, Cosima: see Cosima Liszt
Bülow, Daniela von 12, 30, 32; *13, 15, 22, 31, 54*
Bülow, Eduard von *12*
Bülow, Franziska von 12
Bülow, Isidore von 56

Subject Index

Numbers refer to pages in this book.

About the Author, Editor, and Translator

AUTHOR AND EDITOR

Hans-Joachim Hinrichsen became professor for musicology at the University of Zurich in 1999, after studying German literature, history, and musicology, and teaching at Berlin's *Freie Universität*. His main fields of research are the history of music in the eighteenth through twentieth centuries, the history of how music is received, the history of musical interpretation, and the aesthetics of music. He is coeditor of the journals *Archiv für Musikwissenschaft* (Archive for Musicology) and *Schubert: Perspektiven* (Schubert: Perspectives), a member of the Academia Europaea and the Austrian Academy of the Sciences, and author of *Musikalische Interpretation: Hans von Bülow* (1999).

TRANSLATOR

Cynthia Klohr, PhD, from Royal Oak, Michigan, studied philosophy and literature in Detroit and Heidelberg and now teaches philosophy at universities in Karlsruhe, Germany. She has translated books and essays in philosophy, psychology, the theory and history of science, and music.